INCREDIBLE
COMPARISONS

INCREDIBLE
COMPARISONS

Written by
RUSSELL ASH

DORLING KINDERSLEY
LONDON • NEW YORK • STUTTGART • MOSCOW

A DORLING KINDERSLEY BOOK

Art Editors Dominic Zwemmer
and Dorian Spencer Davies
Project Editor Patrick Newman
Editor Tim Hetherington
Deputy Art Director Miranda Kennedy
Deputy Editorial Director Sophie Mitchell
Illustrations Russell Barnett and Richard Bonson
Additional Illustrations Michael Courtney
and Angaelika Elsbach
Production Charlotte Traill

First published in Great Britain in 1996
by Dorling Kindersley Limited,
9 Henrietta Street, London WC2E 8PS

Reprinted 1997

A CIP catalogue record for this book is available
from the British Library

ISBN-07513-5421-X

Reproduced in Great Britain by Dot Gradations Limited, Essex
Printed and bound in Italy by L.E.G.O., Vicenza

CONTENTS

HOW TO USE THIS BOOK

FROM AN EARLY AGE, people with enquiring minds ask such questions as "How big is it?" or "How fast is it?" But even when we learn the answers, it is often hard to grasp what they really mean, especially when dealing with the extraordinary or the unfamiliar. We really want to know how things compare with the commonplace – with the weight of a human, the speed of a car, or the height of a house. *Incredible Comparisons* makes just such comparisons. This is more than a book of record-breakers, however – there are plenty of averages too. Also, of course, records such as the highest high jump and the tallest building are often broken – but the world's highest mountain will always be just that. Also, while most of the comparisons in the book are between real things, with the illustrations we are able to do things that are impossible in real life. We turn a mountain upside down, lay rail track on Mars, and invite the entire population of the world to move to Bali. By turning the pages, you can join in this exploration of the multitude of comparisons that shape both our world and other worlds beyond.

TURNING THE PAGES

Each time you turn a page of the book you will find a new section on a new topic. Most sections cover two pages, but some open out into four. The section shown here, on *Growth and age*, is two pages.

Averaging out the people

Throughout the book, various things are compared with average size people of different ages. For example, the average two-year-old boy is given to be 84 cm (2 ft 9 in) tall and to weigh 11.8 kg (26 lb).

ABBREVIATIONS USED IN THIS BOOK				
mm	=	millimetre	°F	=	degrees Fahrenheit
cm	=	centimetre	in	=	inch
m	=	metre	ft	=	foot
km	=	kilometre	oz	=	ounce
kph	=	kilometres per hour	lb	=	pound
g	=	gram	mph	=	miles per hour
kg	=	kilogram	sq	=	square
°C	=	degrees Celsius	%	=	per cent

LARGE NUMBERS		
1,000,000	=	One million (One thousand thousand)
1,000,000,000	=	One billion (One thousand million)
1,000,000,000,000	=	One trillion (One million million)

WEIGHTS AND MEASURES		
1 cm	=	10 mm
1 m	=	100 cm
1 km	=	1,000 m
1 kg	=	1,000 g
1 tonne	=	1,000 kg
1 litre	=	1,000 cubic cm
1 lb	=	16 oz
1 ton	=	2,240 lb
1 ft	=	12 in
1 mile	=	5,280 ft

Talking point

Look out for the voice caption, which appears somewhere in nearly every section of the book – although you are not always able to see who is doing the talking!

For real

Some of the comparisons in the book are real. This one shows a kind of deep-sea clam that takes 100 years to grow as big as your fingernail.

True size

Some things in the book, such as this baby kangaroo, are shown actual size. A caption tells you when this is the case.

Scales of comparison

In nearly every section of the book there is at least one horizontal or vertical scale, showing such things as the speed, size, and distance of various objects. This way you can make instant, at-a-glance comparisons between the different objects. The horizontal scale here shows how long various trees and animals live.

Moving from page to page

Several familiar objects, such as the Statue of Liberty, shown here, appear on different pages throughout the book. They allow you to make your own comparisons between objects on different pages. Here, the Statue of Liberty stands alongside the world's tallest tree and a single strand of Pacific giant kelp, a kind of seaweed.

Imaginary comparisons

Some of the comparisons in the book are imaginary. For example, this one shows that you would grow up to be as big as an adult blue whale if you were to grow at the same rate as a kangaroo.

Speed for speed

The French *TGV* train, Concorde, and the X-15A-2 aircraft are among the vehicles that feature regularly in the book. In addition to straightforward speed comparisons, they are used to express long distances in terms of journey times.

French *TGV* train: fastest scheduled speed 246 kph (153 mph)

Concorde: cruising speed 2,179 kph (1,354 mph)

X-15A-2: maximum speed 7,297 kph (4,534 mph)

Square by square

Throughout the book, different surface areas are shown as different size squares. The larger the square, the bigger the surface area. In this example, the squares show the surface areas of different planets. Surface areas are also regularly compared with the area of one or more tennis courts.

Neptune: surface area about 8,024,000,000 sq km (3,098,308,700 sq miles)

Uranus: surface area about 8,209,000,000 sq km (3,169,742,800 sq miles)

Saturn: surface area about 45,644,000,000 sq km (17,624,526,000 sq miles)

Jupiter: surface area about 65,039,000,000 sq km (25,113,522,000 sq miles)

Tennis court: 261 sq m (2,808 sq ft)

By the tubful

Standard bathtub: 80 litres (17.5 gallons)

Volumes of water and other liquids are sometimes given in the book as the number of bathtubs they could fill.

Very large volumes

Very large volumes – such as all the water in the Indian Ocean – are shown as different size cubes. The larger the cube, the bigger the volume.

Indian Ocean: 284,000,000 cubic km (68,000,000 cubic miles)

From place to place

Lengths and distances in the book are often compared to the distances between cities. Here the Amazon River is compared to the distance between New York and Berlin.

New York

Berlin

Amazon River

Holding hands all in a line

One way lengths and distances are expressed in the book is in number of people holding hands. About 1.2 m (4 ft) is allowed for each person.

Great Wall of China

Height and depth

Buildings and other objects are used throughout the book to show heights and depths. Some of them are shown here.

Four-storey town house: height 20 m (66 ft)

Empire State Building: height 381 m (1,250 ft)

Eiffel Tower: height 321 m (1,052 ft)

Saturn V rocket: height 111 m (364 ft)

Versatile jumbo

Different facts about Boeing 747 jumbo jets are used to make a variety of comparisons throughout the book.

Cruising speed: 978 kph (608 mph)

Length: 70.4 m (231 ft)

747

BOEING 747

Maximum passenger capacity: 570

Wingspan: 59.6 m (195.5 ft)

Thrust: 101,560 kg (223,898 lb)

Fuel capacity: 217,000 litres (47,734 gallons)

Weighty matters

In the book, the weights of different things are compared with the weights of a variety of objects, including a fully grown blue whale and an adult bull African elephant.

A fully grown blue whale might weigh 130 tonnes (128 tons) – or about the same as 26 adult bull African elephants.

An adult bull African elephant weighs about 5 tonnes (5 tons).

ON THE SURFACE

ALL THE LAND on Earth makes up only 29 per cent of the planet's surface – the rest is sea. Three-quarters of all land is forest, desert, and pasture. Most of the rest is farmland, or is under ice. Mountains account for a very small area – towns and cities even less. If you scooped up the largest desert – the Sahara Desert, in northern Africa – and dumped it on the other side of the Atlantic Ocean, it would completely cover the US mainland. Even the tallest skyscrapers would be buried under the massive sand dunes of the Sahara.

Turning forest into farmland

The surface area of Earth totals about 510,000,000 sq km (196,926,400 sq miles). Of that, just 149,200,000 sq km (57,610,626 sq miles) is land. After centuries of clearing trees – for timber, mining, and new farmland – forest still covers the largest part.

Forest	39,000,000 sq km (15,059,077 sq miles)	26 per cent of total land area
Desert	35,300,000 sq km (13,630,396 sq miles)	24 per cent of total land area
Pasture	34,200,000 sq km (13,205,652 sq miles)	23 per cent of total land area
Icecap	15,000,000 sq km (5,791,953 sq miles)	10 per cent of total land area
Cultivated	14,400,000 sq km (5,560,275 sq miles)	10 per cent of total land area
Other	11,300,000 sq km (4,363,271 sq miles)	7 per cent of total land area

Forest | Desert | Pasture | Icecap | Cultivated | Other

Cross-country by *TGV*

Travelling at its fastest scheduled speed of 246 kph (153 mph), the French *TGV*, or High Speed Train, would take under four hours to cover a distance equal to the widest part of its home country. It would take the same train almost 10 times as long, however, to cover a distance equal to the widest part of the largest country in the world, Russia.

France occupies an area of 515,000 sq km (198,857 sq miles). At its widest it measures 974 km (605 miles). The *TGV* could cover this distance in just three hours and 58 minutes.

Vatican not so vast

A state within a state, the tiny Vatican City, in Italy, occupies just 0.44 sq km (0.17 sq miles) – about the same area as 60 soccer pitches, each being 100 m (328 ft) long and 73 m (239.5 ft) wide.

Outsized island

Greenland is the largest island on Earth, covering a total area of 2,175,600 sq km (840,065 sq miles). It is three times as big as Borneo, the second largest island in the world, and nine times as big as Honshu, the main island of Japan. Greenland belongs to Denmark, but if it were a separate country it would actually be the thirteenth largest country in the world.

Honshu, Japan: 230,448 sq km (88,983 sq miles)

Borneo: 744,366 sq km (287,422 sq miles)

Greenland: 2,175,600 sq km (840,065 sq miles)

Covering an area of 2,505,813 sq km (967,570 sq miles), Sudan is the largest country in Africa. At its widest it measures 1,850 km (1,150 miles) – a distance equivalent to a *TGV* journey time of seven hours and 31 minutes.

Australia covers 7,836,848 sq km (3,026,044 sq miles). At its widest it is 3,983 km (2,475 miles) from coast to coast. This is equivalent to a *TGV* journey time of 16 hours and 12 minutes.

I'm nearly there! If I were crossing Russia, however, I wouldn't even have reached the halfway point yet.

The total area of the USA (including Alaska and Hawaii) is 9,529,063 sq km (3,679,459 sq miles). At its widest, the USA is 4,517 km (2,807 miles) from coast to coast – equivalent to a *TGV* journey time of 18 hours and 22 minutes.

Russia is far and away the largest country on Earth, covering 17,075,400 sq km (6,593,328 sq miles). At its widest, Russia is a cross-country journey of 9,650 km (5,996 miles). It would take the *TGV* 39 hours and 14 minutes to cover this distance.

0 | 1,000 km (621 miles) | 2,000 km (1,243 miles) | 3,000 km (1,864 miles) | 4,000 km (2,486 miles)

Unbroken border

The longest unbroken frontier in the world – between Canada and the USA – stretches 6,416 km (3,987 miles). This is slightly longer than the Great Wall of China, which totals about 6,400 km (3,977 miles). Allowing some 1.2 m (4 ft) per person, this is equivalent to a line of some 5,300,000 people holding hands.

Fly me to the Moon

The total length of all the world's coastlines is not far short of the average distance between Earth and the Moon. Even at Concorde's supersonic cruising speed of 2,179 kph (1,354 mph) it would take you a week to fly this far.

The total length of all the world's coastlines is reckoned to be about 356,000 km (221,214 miles).

Concorde

The average distance between Earth and the Moon is 384,000 km (238,613 miles).

The border between Canada and the USA is longer than the Great Wall of China.

Each figure represents about 10,000 people.

A decade of deforestation

Clearing tropical rainforest causes loss of valuable plant and animal species, destruction of tribal peoples' ways of life, increased soil erosion, and possibly even global warming. Worldwide, in the 1980s, some 1,541,000 sq km (585,027 sq miles) of rainforest were cleared – about eight per cent of the total area.

Asia and the Pacific: 390,000 sq km (150,591 sq miles) of rainforest lost in the 1980s

Africa: 410,000 sq km (158,313 sq miles) lost in the 1980s

Overall, an area of rainforest larger than Alaska was cleared in the 1980s.

South America and the Caribbean: 741,000 sq km (286,122 sq miles) lost in the 1980s

Asia is biggest

Of the seven continents, the largest, Asia, accounts for almost a third of all the land on Earth.

Europe: 10,000,000 sq km (3,861,302 sq miles) – 7% of the world's land

Oceania: 9,000,000 sq km (3,475,172 sq miles) – 6% of the world's land

Antarctica: 14,000,000 sq km (5,405,823 sq miles) – 9.5% of the world's land

South America: 18,000,000 sq km (6,950,344 sq miles) – 12% of the world's land

North America: 24,000,000 sq km (9,267,125 sq miles) – 16% of the world's land

Africa: 30,000,000 sq km (11,583,906 sq miles) – 20% of the world's land

Asia: 44,000,000 sq km (16,989,728 sq miles) – 29.5% of the world's land

Desert lands that compare to whole countries

About a quarter of all land is desert. Some deserts are semi-arid. Other deserts are extremely arid, with almost no rainfall at all. The Australian Desert is bigger than India, yet it is less than half as big as the enormous Sahara Desert, in northern Africa.

The Kalahari Desert, in southern Africa, covers 520,000 sq km (200,788 sq miles) – an area bigger than France.

Covering 1,040,000 sq km (401,575 sq miles), the Gobi Desert is the largest desert in Asia.

At 1,300,000 sq km (501,969 sq miles), the Arabian Desert is bigger than Peru.

The Australian Desert covers 3,800,000 sq km (1,467,295 sq miles).

The Sahara Desert is the largest desert in the world, covering 9,065,000 sq km (3,500,270 sq miles).

Mountains of desert sand

The world's tallest sand dunes are found in the Sahara. They are big enough to bury big buildings such as the Great Pyramid, in Egypt, and the Eiffel Tower, in Paris.

Some sand dunes in the African Sahara are 465 m (1,526 ft) tall – more than 23 times as tall as a four-storey town house.

Four-storey town house: 20 m (66 ft)

Eiffel Tower: 321 m (1,052 ft)

Great Pyramid: 147 m (481 ft)

An Eiffel lot of ice

The icecap over the South Pole is some 2,800 m (9,186 ft) thick – almost as deep as a stack of nine Eiffel Towers. Incredibly, in some places the Antarctic icecap is 4,780 m (15,682 ft) thick – almost as deep as 15 Eiffel Towers.

Icecap over South Pole: 2,800 m (9,186 ft)

Nine Eiffel Towers: 2,889 m (9,478 ft)

A desert as big as the USA

The Sahara Desert extends across northern Africa. With large expanses receiving little or no rain for years at a time, and an average annual temperature of 27°C (80°F), it is an inhospitable region supporting fewer than 2,000,000 people, mostly on its relatively fertile margins. The Sahara covers an area about the size of mainland USA. The population of the USA is more than 130 times as big, however. Only three countries in the world are bigger than the Sahara Desert: Russia, Canada, and China.

The Sahara Desert could cover the whole of mainland USA.

6,000 km (3,728 miles)　　7,000 km (4,350 miles)　　8,000 km (4,971 miles)　　9,000 km (5,592 miles)　　10,000 km (6,214 miles)

3,000 m
(9,843 ft)

INTO THE EARTH

VIEWED FROM SPACE, through the window of an orbiting spacecraft, the Earth appears to be completely smooth, like a multicoloured beachball – yet the surface of our planet is pitted with craters, scored with canyons, and riddled with caves. The deepest hole ever drilled is deeper than the deepest canyon – yet it does not even break through the Earth's crust, which covers the interior of the planet like the skin of a giant apple.

Colossal craters

Sudbury Crater, in Ontario, Canada, is 140 km (87 miles) wide. It is the largest crater on Earth. There are much bigger craters on the Moon, however – all of them made by meteorites. Bailly Crater, for example, is nearly as wide as the distance from Paris to London.

2,500 m
(8,202 ft)

Chasmic canyons

Canyons are very deep, very narrow valleys, with very steep – almost vertical – sides. They are usually found in hot, dry places, where soft or weak rock is rapidly worn through by rivers, but where there is not enough rain to wash away the sides of the river valleys. The great canyons of the USA are the most spectacular of all. At its deepest point, Kings Canyon, in California, is deep enough to swallow a stack of six-and-a-half Empire State Buildings.

London

Bailly Crater is the largest crater on the near side of the Moon. On the dark side, however, the Orientale Basin is three times as large.

2,000 m
(6,562 ft)

The Snake River has gouged out Hells Canyon, in Oregon and Idaho, to a maximum depth of 2,408 m (7,900 ft) – more than three-and-a-half times as deep as the deepest point in the North Sea.

Kings Canyon: maximum depth 2,499 m (8,199 ft)

Caves top canyons

One of the true wonders of the natural world, the mighty Grand Canyon is more than twice as long as Hells Canyon, and nine times as long as Kings Canyon. The combined length of all the caves in the Mammoth Cave system, in Kentucky, in the USA, is even greater, however.

Empire State Building, New York: 381 m (1,250 ft) tall

1,500 m
(4,921 ft)

Solid as a rock?

The Earth's crust consists of solid rock, but if you were to break it down into its component elements, nearly half of it would vanish into thin air! This is because almost half of the Earth's crust is made up of just one element – oxygen.

Hello down there! I'm nearly half-way down, but I'm still more than three times as high up as the top of the Empire State Building.

The Grand Canyon, in Arizona, was formed by the Colorado River, and has a maximum depth of 1,600 m (5,249 ft) – equivalent to a stack of 80 four-storey town houses.

1,000 m
(3,281 ft)

Oxygen: 46.6%

Silicon: 27.7%

Aluminium: 8.1%

Kings Canyon is in the Sierra Nevada mountains. Unlike Hells Canyon and the Grand Canyon, which were formed solely by river erosion, Kings Canyon was formed by a combination of river erosion and erosion by glaciers.

Sodium: 2.8%

Iron: 5%

Calcium: 3.6%

Potassium: 2.6%

Magnesium: 2.1%

Hydrogen: 1%

Titanium: 0.5%

500 m
(1,640 ft)

The North Sea has a maximum depth of 660 m (2,165 ft). Its average depth, however, is only 94 m (308 ft).

Four-storey town house: 20 m (66 ft)

0

GOING INTO SPACE

"THREE... TWO... ONE... We have lift-off!" Your seat vibrates, and you start moving upwards, slowly at first, then ever faster. You are on board the world's most powerful vehicle, being thrust into space with the force of 31 jumbo jets. The ride is surprisingly smooth, however – some rollercoasters push you harder into your seat – so you hardly realize you are travelling 10 times faster than a rifle bullet. In orbit, you have a unique view of Earth, floating in the vastness of space. With luck, you might spot a mighty comet the size of France, with a tail as long as five planets. But watch out for meteorites. At orbital velocity, a plum-sized meteorite can do as much damage as a speeding car.

Wind speeds on Neptune, which has an atmosphere of mainly hydrogen, reach 2,000 kph (1,243 mph) – 10 times as fast as the strongest tropical storms on Earth.

| 0 | 1,500 kph (932 mph) | 5,000 kph (3,107 mph) |

The speed of sound through air at ground level on Earth is 1,229 kph (764 mph).

Space is the place for speed

Friction restricts the speed of objects through air. But space is a near vacuum, so probes such as *Helios B* travel many times faster than any object through air. Even the planets move at quite high speeds as they orbit the Sun. The only thing that travels faster through air than through space is sound. The speed of sound in space is zero, because sound cannot travel in a vacuum – space is completely silent.

Standing tall on the launch pad

Launchers at the Kennedy Space Center, in Florida, in the USA, tower over the surrounding marshland. The *Saturn V* rockets, used for the *Apollo* Moon missions in the 1960s and early 1970s, were as tall as a 30-storey building. At lift-off, even a space shuttle is as tall as the Leaning Tower of Pisa, in Italy.

Cargo space

A space shuttle is a freighter, with a cargo bay big enough to hold a humpback whale – with room to spare for 1,000 or so herring. Alternatively, you could fill it with 250,000 chocolate bars, each weighing 118 g (4 oz).

The cargo bay of a space shuttle is 18.3 m (60 ft) long, and can hold up to 29.5 tonnes (29 tons). A fully grown humpback whale is about 15 m (49 ft) long and weighs about 29 tonnes (28.5 tons).

Shuttle power

At lift-off, a space shuttle comprises a huge external fuel tank and two solid-fuel rocket boosters as well as the familiar orbiter, and is almost 31 times as powerful as a Boeing 747 jumbo jet. This is because a space shuttle must quickly accelerate to a staggering 28,000 kph (17,400 mph) – nearly four times as fast as the world's fastest ever plane, the X-15A-2 – to get into orbit above the Earth's atmosphere.

31 jumbo jets: combined thrust 3,148,360 kg (6,940,829 lb)

Space shuttle at lift-off: 56 m (184 ft) tall 3,140,920 kg (6,924,427 lb) thrust

Boeing 747 jumbo jet: 70.4 m (231 ft) long 101,560 kg (223,898 lb) thrust

External fuel tank

Solid-fuel rocket booster

Orbiter

Saturn V rocket (1973): 111 m (364 ft)

110 m (361 ft)
100 m (328 ft)
90 m (295 ft)
80 m (262 ft)
70 m (230 ft)
60 m (197 ft)
50 m (164 ft)
40 m (131 ft)
30 m (98 ft)
20 m (66 ft)
10 m (33 ft)
0

External fuel tank

Orbiter

Solid-fuel rocket booster

At take-off, the total height of a space shuttle, including the orbiter, expendable external fuel tank, and two reusable solid-fuel rocket boosters, is 56 m (184 ft).

European *Ariane IV* rocket (1988): 58.4 m (192 ft)

I don't think I'll go right up to the top – it feels a bit wobbly up here! Just imagine how those Apollo guys felt, waiting for blast-off way up there on top of those Saturn Vs!

Russian *Soyuz A2* rocket (1995): 49.5 m (162 ft)

Leaning Tower of Pisa: 55 m (180 ft)

Compact probe

Space capsules, satellites, and probes are tiny compared with the powerful rocket and shuttle launchers that propel them out of the Earth's atmosphere and into space. The *Giotto* space probe, which flew past Halley's Comet in 1986, was about the same size as a small car.

Giotto space probe: 3.1 m (10 ft)

Collision course

Giotto scientists knew that debris pouring off Halley's Comet would eventually destroy the probe – but not before it had beamed invaluable photographs and data back to Earth.

Giotto: 3.1 m (10 ft)

THE SOLAR SYSTEM

AS AN ASTRONAUT on the first voyage to another planet, what should you pack? Let's start with the essentials: don't forget your toothbrush. Actually, you had better pack several – it is a two-year round trip to even the nearest planet to Earth, Mars. What about clothes? Your space suit comes courtesy of the space agency, but you will need casual wear as well. If you are heading away from the Sun, be sure to wrap up warm on the planets beyond Mars, because they are all colder than Antarctica. Venus is warmer, but you can leave your swim-suit behind: you will need a fire-fighter's outfit to survive the searing heat. For the smaller planets, take your trainers. You can look forward to some fun, especially if you were always the last to be picked for the basketball team. On Mars you will be able to jump three times as high as you can on Earth. The bad news is that, under Martian rules, the hoop must be 9 m (30 ft) off the ground.

Earth: average distance from the Sun 149,600,000 km (92,959,671 miles)

Mars: average distance from the Sun 227,940,000 km (141,639,220 miles)

Sun

Mercury: average distance from the Sun 57,910,000 km (35,984,589 miles)

250,000,000 km (155,347,040 miles)

Venus: average distance from the Sun 108,200,000 km (67,234,201 miles)

Pluto keeps its distance

Pluto is the most distant planet. If the Sun were your head, and you whirled Earth around it on the end of a string, you would need a string 40 times as long for Pluto.

Pluto has an equatorial diameter of 2,324 km (1,444 miles). Its one moon, Charon, is 1,270 km (789 miles) wide.

Mercury is 4,878 km (3,031 miles) wide.

Mars has an equatorial diameter of 6,794 km (4,222 miles). It has two tiny moons: Phobos and Deimos.

Venus is 12,104 km (7,521 miles) wide.

The Moon is 3,477 km (2,161 miles) wide.

Earth is 12,756 km (7,926 miles) wide.

Triton

Neptune has an equatorial diameter of 50,538 km (31,404 miles). It has eight moons: the largest, Triton, is 2,705 km (1,681 miles) wide.

Uranus is 51,118 km (31,764 miles) wide at its equator. It has 15 moons: the largest, Titania, is 1,578 km (981 miles) wide.

Titania

Titan

Saturn has an equatorial diameter of 120,536 km (74,900 miles). It has 18 moons: the largest, Titan, is 5,150 km (3,200 miles) wide.

Jupiter is 143,884 km (89,408 miles) wide at its equator. It has 16 moons: the largest, Ganymede, is 5,268 km (3,273 miles) wide.

Ganymede

Ripened by the Sun?

The nine planets orbiting the Sun are as varied in size as the different fruits and vegetables that we eat – the smallest planets are smaller than some of the moons of other planets. If Venus and Earth were plums, Mars would be a gooseberry, Mercury a grape, and Pluto a pea. Neptune and Uranus would be grapefruits, while Saturn and Jupiter would be watermelons. On the same scale, the Sun would be enormous – equivalent to a circular dining table big enough to seat 20 people.

Sizing up the Moon

You can cover the Moon in the sky with a coin held at arm's length. In fact, it is a quarter as wide as Earth, and nearly as wide as Australia.

Earth is 12,756 km (7,926 miles) wide.

The Moon is 3,477 km (2,161 miles) wide.

Australia is 3,983 km (2,475 miles) wide at its widest.

Planetary bulges

None of the nine planets is a perfect sphere – they all bulge at their equators, and are flattened at their poles.

The Sun's diameter is 1,392,140 km (865,059 miles).

Greetings, Earthlings! This space suit felt really heavy back on Earth, but here on the Moon you hardly know you've got it on, and you can leap around all over the place!

On the Moon, an astronaut in a space suit weighs about 22 kg (48 lb).

On Earth, an astronaut in a space suit weighs about 135 kg (298 lb).

Less weighty matters

The less massive the planet or moon, the weaker its gravity. The Moon's gravity is a sixth of that of Earth. On the Moon, therefore, you would weigh a sixth of what you do on Earth, and a single bound would send you soaring.

Holding hands to better understand

The Sun and planets are so large that their sizes are hard to grasp. One way to understand how big they are is to imagine them ringed by people holding hands. Allowing about 1.2 m (4 ft) for each person, the Sun is so enormous that it would take more people than there are in Asia to encircle it. Saturn would take nearly everyone in South America, while Earth would need more people than there are in the whole of Canada. Even Pluto would need about the entire population of Hong Kong.

It would take about 316,000,000 people holding hands to ring the 378,675-km (235,304-mile) equator of Saturn.

It would take about 33,000,000 people holding hands to go around the 40,075-km (24,902-mile) equator of Earth.

It would take about 6,000,000 people holding hands to encircle the 7,300-km (4,536-mile) equator of Pluto.

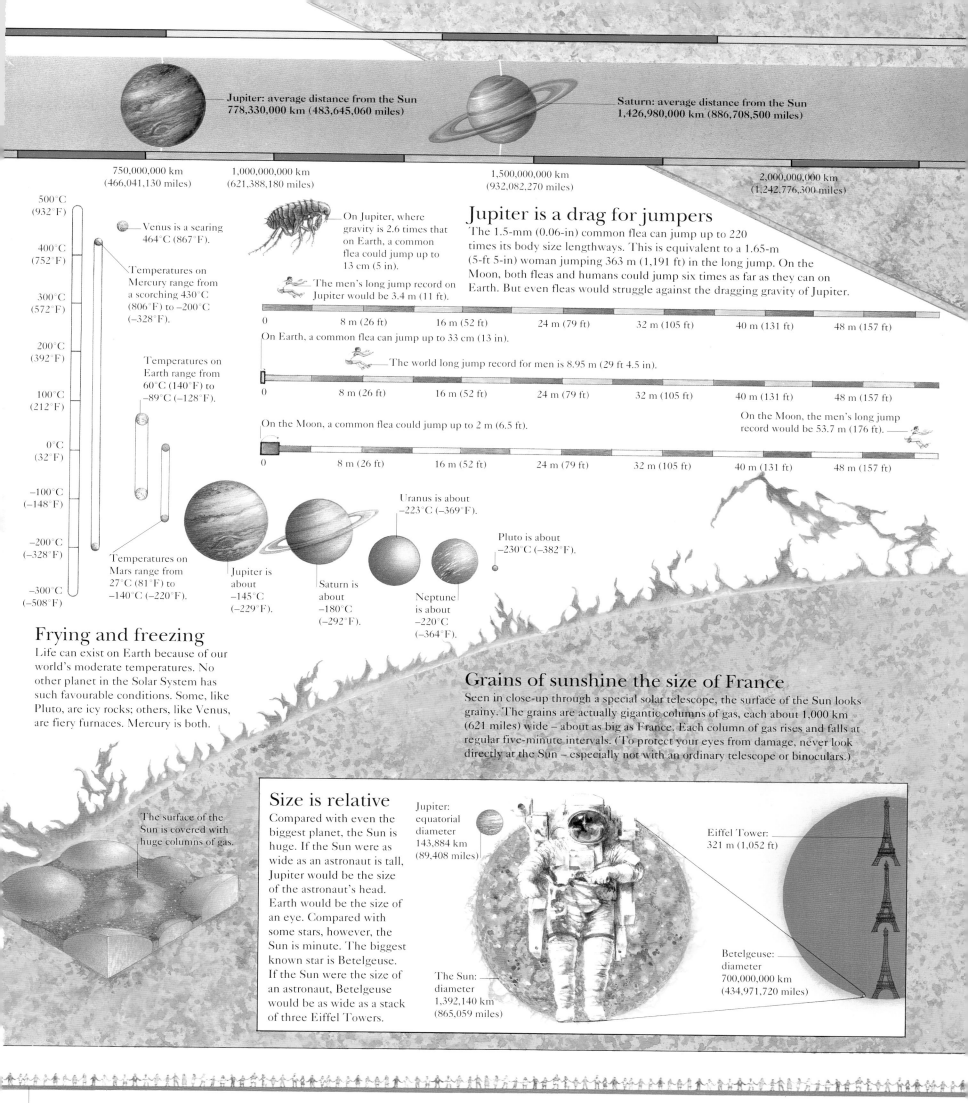

Jupiter: average distance from the Sun
778,330,000 km (483,645,060 miles)

Saturn: average distance from the Sun
1,426,980,000 km (886,708,500 miles)

750,000,000 km
(466,041,130 miles)

1,000,000,000 km
(621,388,180 miles)

1,500,000,000 km
(932,082,270 miles)

2,000,000,000 km
(1,242,776,300 miles)

500°C
(932°F)

400°C
(752°F)

300°C
(572°F)

200°C
(392°F)

100°C
(212°F)

0°C
(32°F)

−100°C
(−148°F)

−200°C
(−328°F)

−300°C
(−508°F)

Venus is a searing
464°C (867°F).

Temperatures on
Mercury range from
a scorching 430°C
(806°F) to −200°C
(−328°F).

Temperatures on
Earth range from
60°C (140°F) to
−89°C (−128°F).

Temperatures on
Mars range from
27°C (81°F) to
−140°C (−220°F).

On Jupiter, where
gravity is 2.6 times that
on Earth, a common
flea could jump up to
13 cm (5 in).

The men's long jump record on
Jupiter would be 3.4 m (11 ft).

Jupiter is a drag for jumpers

The 1.5-mm (0.06-in) common flea can jump up to 220
times its body size lengthways. This is equivalent to a 1.65-m
(5-ft 5-in) woman jumping 363 m (1,191 ft) in the long jump. On the
Moon, both fleas and humans could jump six times as far as they can on
Earth. But even fleas would struggle against the dragging gravity of Jupiter.

| 0 | 8 m (26 ft) | 16 m (52 ft) | 24 m (79 ft) | 32 m (105 ft) | 40 m (131 ft) | 48 m (157 ft) |

On Earth, a common flea can jump up to 33 cm (13 in).

The world long jump record for men is 8.95 m (29 ft 4.5 in).

| 0 | 8 m (26 ft) | 16 m (52 ft) | 24 m (79 ft) | 32 m (105 ft) | 40 m (131 ft) | 48 m (157 ft) |

On the Moon, a common flea could jump up to 2 m (6.5 ft).

On the Moon, the men's long jump
record would be 53.7 m (176 ft).

| 0 | 8 m (26 ft) | 16 m (52 ft) | 24 m (79 ft) | 32 m (105 ft) | 40 m (131 ft) | 48 m (157 ft) |

Uranus is about
−223°C (−369°F).

Pluto is about
−230°C (−382°F).

Jupiter is
about
−145°C
(−229°F).

Saturn is
about
−180°C
(−292°F).

Neptune
is about
−220°C
(−364°F).

Frying and freezing

Life can exist on Earth because of our
world's moderate temperatures. No
other planet in the Solar System has
such favourable conditions. Some, like
Pluto, are icy rocks; others, like Venus,
are fiery furnaces. Mercury is both.

Grains of sunshine the size of France

Seen in close-up through a special solar telescope, the surface of the Sun looks
grainy. The grains are actually gigantic columns of gas, each about 1,000 km
(621 miles) wide – about as big as France. Each column of gas rises and falls at
regular five-minute intervals. (To protect your eyes from damage, never look
directly at the Sun – especially not with an ordinary telescope or binoculars.)

The surface of the
Sun is covered with
huge columns of gas.

Size is relative

Compared with even the
biggest planet, the Sun is
huge. If the Sun were as
wide as an astronaut is tall,
Jupiter would be the size
of the astronaut's head.
Earth would be the size of
an eye. Compared with
some stars, however, the
Sun is minute. The biggest
known star is Betelgeuse.
If the Sun were the size of
an astronaut, Betelgeuse
would be as wide as a stack
of three Eiffel Towers.

Jupiter:
equatorial
diameter
143,884 km
(89,408 miles)

Eiffel Tower:
321 m (1,052 ft)

Betelgeuse:
diameter
700,000,000 km
(434,971,720 miles)

The Sun:
diameter
1,392,140 km
(865,059 miles)

It would take about 3,645,000,000 people holding hands to go
around the 4,374,000-km (2,717,952-mile) equator of the Sun.

Each figure represents about 10,000,000 people.

400,000 km (248,555 miles)

500,000 km (310,694 miles)

600,000 km (372,833 miles)

700,000 km (434,972 miles)

Bailly Crater is 303 km (188 miles) wide. This is almost as wide as the distance from London to Paris – 342 km (212 miles).

Paris

If Sudbury Crater were dug up in one piece and transported to the Moon, it would easily fit inside Bailly Crater. It is uncertain whether Sudbury Crater was made by a meteorite, or is an extinct volcano. The largest crater on Earth that was definitely made by a meteorite is the 1,265-m (4,150-ft) wide Barringer Crater, in Arizona.

Borehole barely pricks the skin

The average distance to the centre of the Earth is 6,378 km (3,963 miles). On average, the crust is 24 km (15 miles) thick. The deepest hole ever drilled – at Kola Peninsula, in Russia – is about 12 km (7.5 miles) deep. If the Earth were an apple, and the crust its skin, this hole would not even pierce the skin.

The world's highest mountain, Mt Everest, in the Himalayas, is 8,848 m (29,028 ft) high. The Kola borehole is one-and-a-half times as deep as Mt Everest is high, but does not even break through the Earth's crust.

The Earth's crust varies from 5 km (3 miles) thick in places under the sea to 60 km (37 miles) below some mountains.

The lower mantle is solid.

The outer core is molten metal.

Upper mantle: mostly solid, with a liquid layer

The inner core is a solid ball of intensely hot iron under extreme pressure.

3,000 m (9,843 ft)
6,000 m (19,685 ft)
9,000 m (29,528 ft)
12,000 m (39,370 ft)
15,000 m (49,213 ft)

Western Deep Levels gold mine, South Africa: 3,777 m (12,392 ft)

Oil boreholes rarely extend deeper than 9,100 m (29,856 ft)

In 1970, a geological survey team began to bore a hole at the Kola Peninsula. By April 1992 it was 12,262 m (40,230 ft) deep.

0
120 km (75 miles)   240 km (149 miles)   360 km (224 miles)   480 km (298 miles)

Kings Canyon: 49 km (30 miles)
Hells Canyon: 201 km (125 miles)
Grand Canyon: 446 km (277 miles)
Mammoth Cave system: 567 km (352 miles)

0
120 km (75 miles)   240 km (149 miles)   360 km (224 miles)   480 km (298 miles)

How low can you get?

Some places on Earth lie below sea level, the average level of the surface of the oceans. Known as depressions, they usually result from deformations or folds in the Earth's crust.

Salton Sink, USA: 72 m (236 ft) below sea level

Death Valley, USA: 86 m (282 ft) below sea level

Danakil Depression, Ethiopia: 117 m (384 ft) below sea level

Poluostrov Mangyshlak, Kazakhstan: 132 m (433 ft) below sea level

Qattâra Depression, Egypt: 133 m (436 ft) below sea level

Turfan Depression, Xinjiang, China: 154 m (505 ft) below sea level

Going underground

Even the longest transportation tunnels dug by us humans are quite short when compared with the combined lengths of the caves in the most extensive natural cave systems. The Mammoth Cave system is longer than the world's longest glacier. The only tunnels that even come close are railway tunnels, such as the one under the English Channel, and the combined lengths of the tunnels in metropolitan railway systems, such as the London Underground – less than half of which, however, is actually underground.

Mammoth Cave system: 567 km (352 miles) long

Optimisticeskaya Cave system, Ukraine: 183 km (114 miles) long

Hölloch Cave system, Switzerland: 166 km (103 miles) long

Lambert-Fischer Glacier, Antarctica: 515 km (320 miles) long

London Underground railway system: 408 km (254 miles) long

0
100 km (62 miles)
200 km (124 miles)
300 km (186 miles)
400 km (249 miles)
500 km (311 miles)

English Channel railway tunnel from the UK to France: 50 km (31 miles) long

Jewel Cave system, South Dakota, USA: 162 km (101 miles) long

Sea below sea level

The lowest place on Earth is the shoreline of the Dead Sea, which straddles Jordan and Israel. If the Empire State Building were on the shore of the Dead Sea, only the top of its mast would be above sea level.

Dead Sea, Jordan and Israel: 400 m (1,312 ft) below sea level

THE UNIVERSE

THE UNIVERSE IS SO INCREDIBLY VAST that measuring it in kilometres (or miles) is meaningless. Instead, we measure it in light years. A light year is the distance that light travels in one year: 9,460,000,000,000 km (5,878,000,000,000 miles). The nearest star to the Sun is more than four light years away. The next nearest galaxy, the Large Magellanic Cloud, is 169,000 light years away – when we look at the Large Magellanic Cloud, we see it as it was 169,000 years ago. Yet some galaxies are billions of light years away – and there are billions of galaxies, many containing billions of stars.

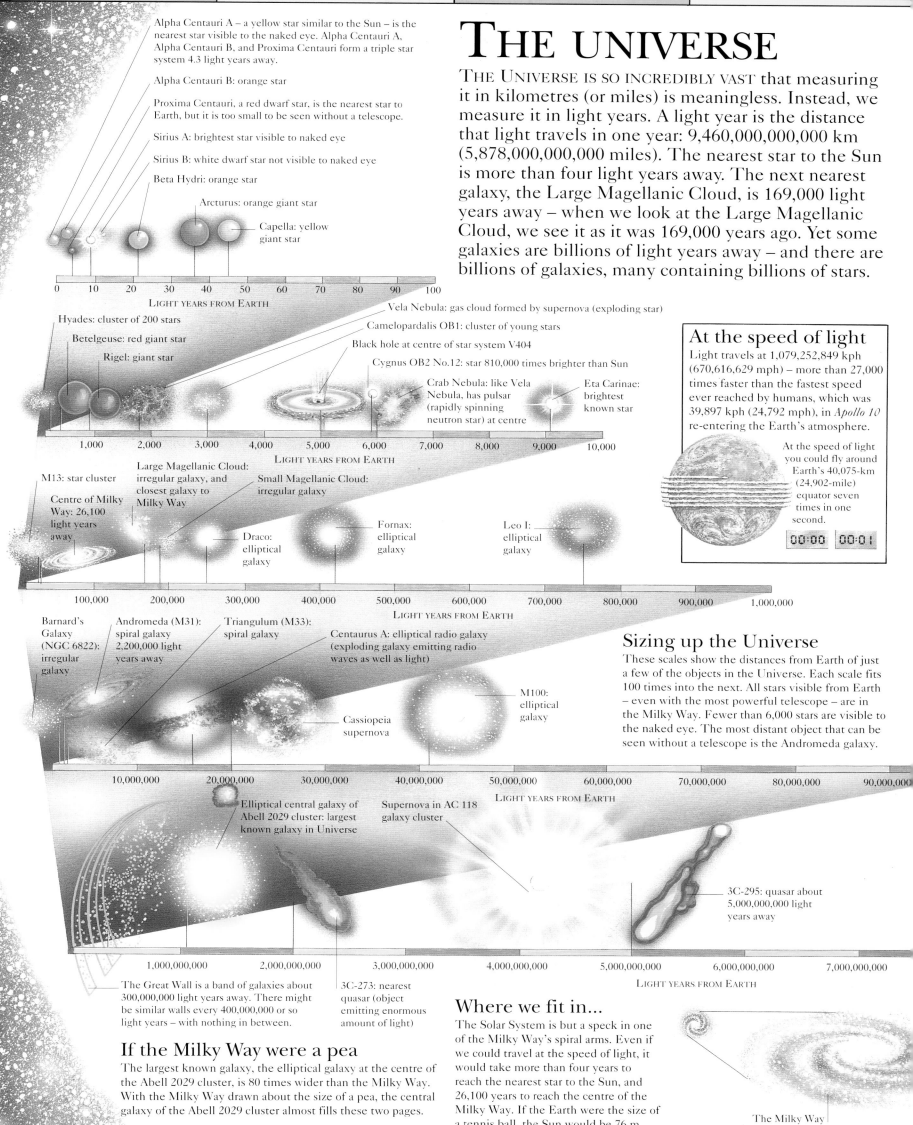

Alpha Centauri A – a yellow star similar to the Sun – is the nearest star visible to the naked eye. Alpha Centauri A, Alpha Centauri B, and Proxima Centauri form a triple star system 4.3 light years away.

Alpha Centauri B: orange star

Proxima Centauri, a red dwarf star, is the nearest star to Earth, but it is too small to be seen without a telescope.

Sirius A: brightest star visible to naked eye

Sirius B: white dwarf star not visible to naked eye

Beta Hydri: orange star

Arcturus: orange giant star

Capella: yellow giant star

0   10   20   30   40   50   60   70   80   90   100
LIGHT YEARS FROM EARTH

Hyades: cluster of 200 stars

Betelgeuse: red giant star

Rigel: giant star

Vela Nebula: gas cloud formed by supernova (exploding star)

Camelopardalis OB1: cluster of young stars

Black hole at centre of star system V404

Cygnus OB2 No.12: star 810,000 times brighter than Sun

Crab Nebula: like Vela Nebula, has pulsar (rapidly spinning neutron star) at centre

Eta Carinae: brightest known star

1,000   2,000   3,000   4,000   5,000   6,000   7,000   8,000   9,000   10,000
LIGHT YEARS FROM EARTH

At the speed of light

Light travels at 1,079,252,849 kph (670,616,629 mph) – more than 27,000 times faster than the fastest speed ever reached by humans, which was 39,897 kph (24,792 mph), in *Apollo 10* re-entering the Earth's atmosphere.

At the speed of light you could fly around Earth's 40,075-km (24,902-mile) equator seven times in one second.

`00:00`   `00:01`

M13: star cluster

Centre of Milky Way: 26,100 light years away

Large Magellanic Cloud: irregular galaxy, and closest galaxy to Milky Way

Draco: elliptical galaxy

Small Magellanic Cloud: irregular galaxy

Fornax: elliptical galaxy

Leo I: elliptical galaxy

100,000   200,000   300,000   400,000   500,000   600,000   700,000   800,000   900,000   1,000,000
LIGHT YEARS FROM EARTH

Barnard's Galaxy (NGC 6822): irregular galaxy

Andromeda (M31): spiral galaxy 2,200,000 light years away

Triangulum (M33): spiral galaxy

Centaurus A: elliptical radio galaxy (exploding galaxy emitting radio waves as well as light)

Cassiopeia supernova

M100: elliptical galaxy

Sizing up the Universe

These scales show the distances from Earth of just a few of the objects in the Universe. Each scale fits 100 times into the next. All stars visible from Earth – even with the most powerful telescope – are in the Milky Way. Fewer than 6,000 stars are visible to the naked eye. The most distant object that can be seen without a telescope is the Andromeda galaxy.

10,000,000   20,000,000   30,000,000   40,000,000   50,000,000   60,000,000   70,000,000   80,000,000   90,000,000
LIGHT YEARS FROM EARTH

Elliptical central galaxy of Abell 2029 cluster: largest known galaxy in Universe

Supernova in AC 118 galaxy cluster

3C-295: quasar about 5,000,000,000 light years away

1,000,000,000   2,000,000,000   3,000,000,000   4,000,000,000   5,000,000,000   6,000,000,000   7,000,000,000
LIGHT YEARS FROM EARTH

The Great Wall is a band of galaxies about 300,000,000 light years away. There might be similar walls every 400,000,000 or so light years – with nothing in between.

3C-273: nearest quasar (object emitting enormous amount of light)

Where we fit in...

The Solar System is but a speck in one of the Milky Way's spiral arms. Even if we could travel at the speed of light, it would take more than four years to reach the nearest star to the Sun, and 26,100 years to reach the centre of the Milky Way. If the Earth were the size of a tennis ball, the Sun would be 76 m (249 ft) away, but the nearest star would still be 20,744 km (12,890 miles) away.

The Milky Way is a spiral galaxy.

If the Milky Way were a pea

The largest known galaxy, the elliptical galaxy at the centre of the Abell 2029 cluster, is 80 times wider than the Milky Way. With the Milky Way drawn about the size of a pea, the central galaxy of the Abell 2029 cluster almost fills these two pages.

The Milky Way is about 100,000 light years wide.

Almost filling both pages, the galaxy at the centre of the Abell 2029 cluster is about 8,000,000 light years wide.

3,000,000,000 km
(1,864,164,500 miles)

3,500,000,000 km
(2,174,858,600 miles)

4,000,000,000 km
(2,485,552,700 miles)

Surface areas

If the surface of Pluto were scaled down to the size of a postage stamp, the surface of Jupiter would be about half the size of a car parking space, while the Sun's surface would cover nearly two tennis courts.

Jupiter: surface area about 65,039,000,000 sq km (25,113,522,000 sq miles)

Neptune: surface area about 8,024,000,000 sq km (3,098,308,700 sq miles)

Uranus: surface area about 8,209,000,000 sq km (3,169,742,800 sq miles)

Saturn: surface area about 45,644,000,000 sq km (17,624,526,000 sq miles)

Pluto: surface area about 17,000,000 sq km (6,564,213 sq miles)

Mercury: surface area about 75,000,000 sq km (28,959,765 sq miles)

Venus: surface area about 460,000,000 sq km (177,619,890 sq miles)

Mars: surface area about 145,000,000 sq km (55,988,879 sq miles)

Earth: surface area about 510,000,000 sq km (196,926,400 sq miles)

Sun: surface area about 6,088,575,000,000 sq km (2,350,982,700,000 sq miles)

A solar prominence can be as long as eight Earths.

Flaming flares

Solar prominences are huge plumes of flame that eject thousands of tonnes of gas into space at hundreds of times the speed of a rifle bullet. They can extend for 100,000 km (62,139 miles) – eight times the width of Earth.

Weighing them up

The five smallest planets are all made mainly of dense rock, and are heavy in proportion to their size. The four largest planets are all made mainly of gas, and are light in proportion to their size. Saturn would actually float in water – if you could find a big enough bowl. Saturn is only slightly smaller than Jupiter, but Jupiter is more than three times as heavy.

Jupiter is as heavy as...

Mars is all dry land

Mars is much smaller than Earth, but, unlike our watery world, is completely dry. In fact, the surface area of Mars is almost as big as the total area of land on Earth. However, dry riverbeds suggest that water did once flow on Mars.

The surface area of Mars is about 145,000,000 sq km (55,988,879 sq miles).

The total area of land on Earth is about 149,200,000 sq km (57,610,626 sq miles).

Sunspots can grow as large as Jupiter.

A watery world

Seen from space, Earth is a blue globe wrapped in cloud. The oceans cover more than two-thirds of the Earth's surface, an area more than large enough to flood the three smallest planets.

The combined surface area of Pluto, Mercury, and Mars is about 237,000,000 sq km (91,512,858 sq miles).

Pluto in perspective

The diameter of the smallest planet, Pluto, is less than the distance between Athens, in Greece, and London. Like most of the planets, Pluto is named after an ancient Greek god.

Pluto is 2,324 km (1,444 miles) wide. The distance between London and Athens is about 2,400 km (1,491 miles).

London

Athens

Mercury

Mars

Pluto

Earth's oceans cover about 360,800,000 sq km (139,315,770 sq miles).

Neptune: average distance from the Sun
4,497,070,000 km (2,794,426,100 miles)

Pluto: average distance from the Sun
5,913,520,000 km (3,674,591,400 miles)

5,000,000,000 km
(3,106,940,900 miles)

5,500,000,000 km
(3,417,634,900 miles)

6,000,000,000 km
(3,728,329,000 miles)

Clay balls

If Jupiter were a huge ball of clay, you could make all the other planets out of it – and still have plenty left over.

The Great Red Spot of Jupiter is 40,000 km (24,856 miles) wide – wider than three Earths.

The volume of Jupiter is about 1,500,000,000,000,000 cubic km (367,021,930,000,000 cubic miles). The combined volume of the other eight planets is only about two-thirds this amount.

Like a huge hurricane

Jupiter has a swirling atmosphere of hydrogen, with weather patterns that can be seen from Earth. The Great Red Spot on Jupiter is a gigantic storm that is more than 300 years old, and more than three times as big as Earth.

A very big valley

Even the great canyons of the USA are minute when compared with the biggest valley on Mars. The Mariner Valley, on Mars, is nine times longer than the Grand Canyon, and three times as deep as Kings Canyon. In fact, it is deep enough and wide enough to swallow the highest peak in South America, Mt Aconcagua.

Mt Aconcagua stands 6,960 m (22,834 ft) high.

Wild is the wind on Neptune

Like Jupiter, Neptune has a violent weather system, with the strongest winds of any planet. Winds on Neptune blow more than four times faster than the most powerful tornado recorded on Earth.

The Mariner Valley is 4,000 km (2,486 miles) long, 75 km (47 miles) wide, and 7,000 m (22,966 ft) deep.

Kings Canyon is 2,449 m (8,199 ft) deep.

Winds on Neptune can reach 2,000 kph (1,243 mph) – more than four times faster than the fastest tornado on Earth.

Tornadoes whirling at up to 450 kph (280 mph) have been recorded on Earth.

...3.3 Saturns

...or 18.5 Neptunes

...or 21.9 Uranuses

...or 317 Earths

...or 393 Venuses

...or 2,894 Marses

...or 5,788 Mercurys

...or 145,796 Plutos.

The Sun's spotty face

The temperature of the Sun's surface is about 5,500°C (9,932°F). Strong magnetic fields sometimes restrict the flow of heat from the Sun's interior, creating slightly cooler, darker surface regions, known as sunspots. Sunspots can last for several months and can grow as large as Jupiter.

It would take more than 100 times as many people holding hands to encircle the Sun as it would to go around the equator of the Earth.

1,100,000 km (683,527 miles)

1,200,000 km (745,666 miles)

1,300,000 km (807,805 miles)

1,400,000 km (869,943 miles)

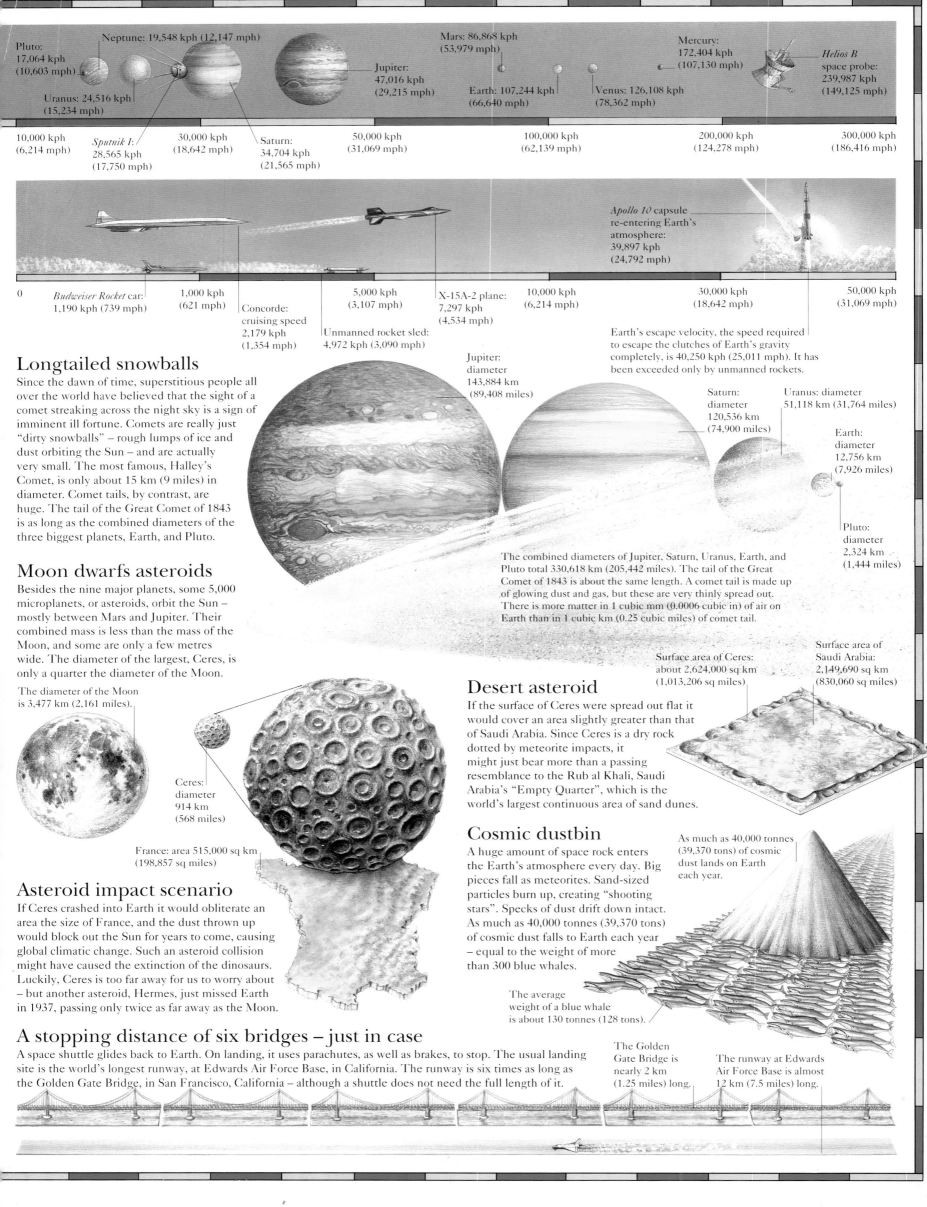

Pluto: 17,064 kph (10,603 mph)

Neptune: 19,548 kph (12,147 mph)

Uranus: 24,516 kph (15,234 mph)

Mars: 86,868 kph (53,979 mph)

Jupiter: 47,016 kph (29,215 mph)

Earth: 107,244 kph (66,640 mph)

Venus: 126,108 kph (78,362 mph)

Mercury: 172,404 kph (107,130 mph)

Helios B space probe: 239,987 kph (149,125 mph)

10,000 kph (6,214 mph)

Sputnik I: 28,565 kph (17,750 mph)

30,000 kph (18,642 mph)

Saturn: 34,704 kph (21,565 mph)

50,000 kph (31,069 mph)

100,000 kph (62,139 mph)

200,000 kph (124,278 mph)

300,000 kph (186,416 mph)

Apollo 10 capsule re-entering Earth's atmosphere: 39,897 kph (24,792 mph)

0

Budweiser Rocket car: 1,190 kph (739 mph)

1,000 kph (621 mph)

Concorde: cruising speed 2,179 kph (1,354 mph)

Unmanned rocket sled: 4,972 kph (3,090 mph)

5,000 kph (3,107 mph)

X-15A-2 plane: 7,297 kph (4,534 mph)

10,000 kph (6,214 mph)

30,000 kph (18,642 mph)

50,000 kph (31,069 mph)

Longtailed snowballs

Since the dawn of time, superstitious people all over the world have believed that the sight of a comet streaking across the night sky is a sign of imminent ill fortune. Comets are really just "dirty snowballs" – rough lumps of ice and dust orbiting the Sun – and are actually very small. The most famous, Halley's Comet, is only about 15 km (9 miles) in diameter. Comet tails, by contrast, are huge. The tail of the Great Comet of 1843 is as long as the combined diameters of the three biggest planets, Earth, and Pluto.

Moon dwarfs asteroids

Besides the nine major planets, some 5,000 microplanets, or asteroids, orbit the Sun – mostly between Mars and Jupiter. Their combined mass is less than the mass of the Moon, and some are only a few metres wide. The diameter of the largest, Ceres, is only a quarter the diameter of the Moon.

The diameter of the Moon is 3,477 km (2,161 miles).

Jupiter: diameter 143,884 km (89,408 miles)

Saturn: diameter 120,536 km (74,900 miles)

Uranus: diameter 51,118 km (31,764 miles)

Earth: diameter 12,756 km (7,926 miles)

Pluto: diameter 2,324 km (1,444 miles)

Earth's escape velocity, the speed required to escape the clutches of Earth's gravity completely, is 40,250 kph (25,011 mph). It has been exceeded only by unmanned rockets.

The combined diameters of Jupiter, Saturn, Uranus, Earth, and Pluto total 330,618 km (205,442 miles). The tail of the Great Comet of 1843 is about the same length. A comet tail is made up of glowing dust and gas, but these are very thinly spread out. There is more matter in 1 cubic mm (0.0006 cubic in) of air on Earth than in 1 cubic km (0.25 cubic miles) of comet tail.

Ceres: diameter 914 km (568 miles)

France: area 515,000 sq km (198,857 sq miles)

Desert asteroid

If the surface of Ceres were spread out flat it would cover an area slightly greater than that of Saudi Arabia. Since Ceres is a dry rock dotted by meteorite impacts, it might just bear more than a passing resemblance to the Rub al Khali, Saudi Arabia's "Empty Quarter", which is the world's largest continuous area of sand dunes.

Surface area of Ceres: about 2,624,000 sq km (1,013,206 sq miles)

Surface area of Saudi Arabia: 2,149,690 sq km (830,060 sq miles)

Asteroid impact scenario

If Ceres crashed into Earth it would obliterate an area the size of France, and the dust thrown up would block out the Sun for years to come, causing global climatic change. Such an asteroid collision might have caused the extinction of the dinosaurs. Luckily, Ceres is too far away for us to worry about – but another asteroid, Hermes, just missed Earth in 1937, passing only twice as far away as the Moon.

Cosmic dustbin

A huge amount of space rock enters the Earth's atmosphere every day. Big pieces fall as meteorites. Sand-sized particles burn up, creating "shooting stars". Specks of dust drift down intact. As much as 40,000 tonnes (39,370 tons) of cosmic dust falls to Earth each year – equal to the weight of more than 300 blue whales.

As much as 40,000 tonnes (39,370 tons) of cosmic dust lands on Earth each year.

The average weight of a blue whale is about 130 tonnes (128 tons).

A stopping distance of six bridges – just in case

A space shuttle glides back to Earth. On landing, it uses parachutes, as well as brakes, to stop. The usual landing site is the world's longest runway, at Edwards Air Force Base, in California. The runway is six times as long as the Golden Gate Bridge, in San Francisco, California – although a shuttle does not need the full length of it.

The Golden Gate Bridge is nearly 2 km (1.25 miles) long.

The runway at Edwards Air Force Base is almost 12 km (7.5 miles) long.

Big Betelgeuse

Stars come in many different sizes. Compared with some stars, the Sun is enormous. Compared with others, it is tiny. The largest known star is the red giant Betelgeuse, some 310 light years away. The diameter of Betelgeuse is about 500 times greater than the diameter of the Sun. If Betelgeuse were the size of a large orange, the Sun would be about the size of the head of a pin.

Betelgeuse: approximate diameter 700,000,000 km (434,971,720 miles)

The Sun: diameter 1,392,140 km (865,059 miles)

A midget among stars

Stars such as the Sun eventually turn into white dwarfs, which are very small, but extremely dense, stars. The Sun is about 250 times wider than the smallest known white dwarf, L362-81, which is almost as small as the Moon.

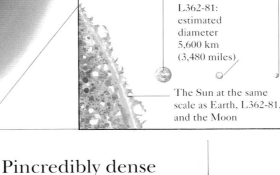

Earth: diameter 12,756 km (7,926 miles)

The Moon: diameter 3,477 km (2,161 miles)

L362-81: estimated diameter 5,600 km (3,480 miles)

The Sun at the same scale as Earth, L362-81, and the Moon

Core cauldron

Like most stars, the Sun is a huge ball of glowing hydrogen. At the Sun's core, the pressure and temperature are so great that hydrogen atoms fuse to make helium. Every second, at its core, the Sun converts about 540,000,000 tonnes (531,496,000 tons) of hydrogen into helium – a weight equal to about 103.5 Great Pyramids.

The Great Pyramid weighs 5,216,400 tonnes (5,134,252 tons) – so 103.5 Great Pyramids would weigh 539,897,400 tonnes (531,395,000 tons).

The Sun

Pincredibly dense

Massive stars such as Betelgeuse eventually turn into neutron stars, which are even smaller and denser than white dwarf stars. A neutron star is so dense that just a pinhead-size amount of one might weigh as much as three Empire State Buildings.

The Empire State Building weighs 331,122 tonnes (325,907 tons) – so three Empire State Buildings would weigh 993,366 tonnes (977,722 tons).

A pinhead-size piece of a neutron star might weigh 1,000,000 tonnes (984,200 tons).

Siriusly heavy

The diameter of the Sun is 144 times greater than the diameter of the white dwarf star Sirius B, which is even smaller than Earth. Sirius B is so dense, however, that it actually weighs more than the Sun, which is itself some 330,000 times heavier than Earth.

The Sun

Sirius B: diameter 9,650 km (5,996 miles)

100,000,000

G2237+0305: quasar

IRAS F10214+4724 is an object 300,000,000,000,000 times brighter than the Sun. It is probably a galaxy.

Some 12,800,000,000 light years distant, radio source 4C41.17 is the remotest known galaxy in the Universe.

PC 1247+3406, a quasar, is about 13,200,000,000 light years away, making it the remotest known object in the Universe.

The observable horizon – the edge of the known Universe – is about 14,000,000,000 light years away.

8,000,000,000 9,000,000,000 10,000,000,000 11,000,000,000 12,000,000,000 13,000,000,000 14,000,000,000 15,000,000,000

The Solar System is located in the Orion Arm of the Milky Way.

Plenty to go around

Nobody knows for sure, but there are an estimated 100,000,000,000 stars in the Milky Way, and about the same number of galaxies in the Universe. That is enough for you and every other person on Earth to stake a claim for 18 of each.

There are an estimated 18 stars in the Milky Way for each person on Earth.

I'll take eight spiral, six elliptical, and four irregular, please.

There are an estimated 18 galaxies in the Universe for each person on Earth.

WATER

WE LIVE IN A WET, wet world. Oceans cover more than two-thirds of our planet's surface. Seen from space, some views of Earth show almost no land at all. The largest ocean, the Pacific, covers nearly a third of the globe and holds about half its water. In fact, 98 per cent of all our world's water is in the sea. Most of the rest is locked up in the two great polar icecaps. Lakes hold just one five-thousandth of our world's water, rivers and streams even less. Clouds hold the least water of all – though you wouldn't think so if you were caught in a tropical rain storm without an umbrella!

Each side of this pool would be about as long as the distance between Perth, in Australia, and New York.

The Moon is 3,477 km (2,161 miles) wide. It would take at least 25 Moons to cover the surface of all the oceans.

Pooled together

Spread out with straight edges, like a swimming pool, all the world's oceans would form a square with sides about 19,000 km (11,806 miles) long – more than five times the diameter of the Moon.

All tanked up

The vast Pacific Ocean contains more water than all the world's other seas and oceans put together. A square tank big enough to hold it would have sides 886 km (551 miles) long.

The Pacific Ocean holds 696,000,000 cubic km (167,000,000 cubic miles) of water.

Lake Nyasa, Malawi/Mozambique: 706 m (2,316 ft)

Lake Baikal: 1,620 m (5,315 ft)

North Sea: 660 m (2,165 ft)

Lake Superior, USA/Canada: 9 m (30 ft)

Plumbing the depths

The world's deepest freshwater lake, Russia's Lake Baikal, reaches 1,620 m (5,315 ft) at its deepest point. The mud at the bottom of the lake is even deeper. Compared with the deepest points in the world's oceans and seas, however, Lake Baikal is shallow. The deepest place on Earth is the Marianas Trench in the Pacific Ocean.

It would take more than 100 Mt Everests stacked on top of one another to reach the surface of this tank.

Gulf of Mexico: 3,787 m (12,425 ft)

South China Sea: 5,016 m (16,456 ft)

Caribbean Sea: 6,946 m (22,788 ft)

Indian Ocean: 7,455 m (24,460 ft)

Present sea level

The Statue of Liberty, in New York, is 93 m (305 ft) high. If all the world's ice melted, poor Liberty would drown – only her torch would show above the waves.

About 71 per cent of the Earth's surface is water.

Only 29 per cent of the Earth's surface is land.

Land and sea

The oceans dominate the Earth's surface, just 29 per cent of which is above sea level. Global warming would reduce the land area still further because melting ice would raise sea levels, flooding low-lying coastal land.

Atlantic Ocean: 9,219 m (30,246 ft)

It would take a stack of 29 Empire State Buildings to reach the surface of the sea from the bottom of the Marianas Trench.

Marianas Trench, Pacific Ocean: 10,918 m (35,820 ft)

Rising damp

Only a small proportion of our world's water is locked up in glaciers and the two polar icecaps, but if they all melted, sea levels would rise dramatically – by about 80 m (262 ft).

On the crest of a wave

Ordinary sea waves are whipped up by the wind. The highest wave ever recorded was in the Pacific Ocean in 1933 and measured 34 m (112 ft) from trough to crest.

Sea tops lake stakes

The landlocked Caspian Sea is the world's largest lake by area, but it is slightly salty. The largest freshwater lake by area is Lake Superior, one of the Great Lakes, in North America.

Lake Baikal: 31,494 sq km (12,160 sq miles)

Aral Sea, Kazakhstan/Uzbekistan: 40,000 sq km (15,444 sq miles)

Lake Victoria, East Africa: 62,940 sq km (24,301 sq miles)

Lake Superior, USA/Canada: 82,260 sq km (31,761 sq miles)

Caspian Sea, Europe/Asia: 378,400 sq km (146,101 sq miles)

The 323,000,000 cubic km (77,000,000 cubic miles) of the Atlantic Ocean would fill a square tank with 686-km (426-mile) sides.

A square tank holding the 284,000,000 cubic km (68,000,000 cubic miles) of the Indian Ocean would need to have sides 657 km (408 miles) long.

Tall fallers

The world's highest waterfall, Angel Falls, in Venezuela, is 979 m (3,212 ft) tall. The longest single drop on the falls is a more modest 807 m (2,648 ft), but that is still more than twice the height of the Eiffel Tower.

Angel Falls, Venezuela: 979 m (3,212 ft)

Utigård, Norway: 800 m (2,625 ft)

Yosemite, USA: 739 m (2,425 ft)

Eiffel Tower: 321 m (1,052 ft)

Sutherland, New Zealand: 580 m (1,903 ft)

Victoria Falls, Zambia/Zimbabwe: 108 m (354 ft)

Niagara Falls, USA/Canada: 51 m (167 ft)

Lake Superior: 12,174 cubic km (2,921 cubic miles)

Lake Baikal: 22,995 cubic km (5,519 cubic miles)

Almost all at sea

Seawater and ice make up 99.35 per cent of all the Earth's water. Almost all of the rest is groundwater stored in porous rocks. Lakes, rivers, and water in the atmosphere make up only 0.0015 per cent of the Earth's water – a quarter of a teaspoonful for each bathful of seawater.

Seawater: 97.2 per cent

Ice: 2.15 per cent

All other water: 0.65 per cent

Owen Falls: 205 cubic km (49 cubic miles)

Aswan, Egypt: 168 cubic km (40 cubic miles)

Guri, Venezuela: 136 cubic km (33 cubic miles)

Zeya, Russia: 68 cubic km (16 cubic miles)

Puddles by comparison

Compared with natural lakes, even the largest artificial reservoirs seem like puny efforts. Lake Baikal, the world's largest freshwater lake by volume, would fill Uganda's Owen Falls, the world's biggest artificial reservoir, 112 times.

Daily output of water from the Amazon

Water in Lake Baikal

Amazing Amazon

The Amazon River, in Brazil, discharges about 10.5 cubic km (2.5 cubic miles) of water a minute into the Atlantic Ocean. That is enough for everyone in the world to have a bath every 44 minutes, allowing 80 litres (17.5 gallons) per bath. If the Amazon drained Lake Baikal, the lake would be two-thirds empty in just one day.

Hidden depths

Although it appears quite small in area, Lake Baikal is extremely deep and contains more water than any other freshwater lake. Lake Superior, the biggest freshwater lake by area, looks bigger, but holds a much smaller volume of water.

Shock waves

Earthquakes and volcanoes can cause especially big waves called tsunamis. The tallest recorded tsunami reached the remarkable height of 85 m (278 ft).

Ahoy there! I'm on this yacht, but I'm so small you can hardly see me.

9,000 m (29,528 ft)

8,000 m (26,247 ft)

7,000 m (22,966 ft)

6,000 m (19,685 ft)

5,000 m (16,404 ft)

4,000 m (13,123 ft)

3,000 m (9,843 ft)

2,000 m (6,562 ft)

1,000 m (3,281 ft)

0

MOUNTAINS

THE WORLD'S HIGHEST natural features, the great mountains, dwarf even the biggest buildings. The tallest mountain of all is Mt Everest, in the Himalayas. The air at the top of Everest is three times as thin as the air at sea level. What with the numbing cold, thin air, and icy rock faces, it takes even the best prepared and most experienced climbers weeks to reach the top of Everest.

On top of the world

The 35 highest mountains in the world are all in the Himalayan and Karakoram ranges, between China and the Indian subcontinent. The top five are Everest, K2, Kanchenjunga, Lhotse I, and Makalu I. Everest is 27 times as high as the Eiffel Tower. An office building the same height would have at least 2,000 floors.

Everest: 8,848 m (29,028 ft)

K2: 8,611 m (28,250 ft)

Kanchenjunga: 8,597 m (28,208 ft)

Lhotse I: 8,511 m (27,923 ft)

Makalu I: 8,481 m (27,824 ft)

At 8,848 m (29,028 ft), Mt Everest towers over the tallest volcanoes. It is half as high again as Mt Kilimanjaro, more than twice as high as Mt Fuji, and nearly seven times as high as Mt Vesuvius.

Mt Kilimanjaro, in Tanzania, rises to 5,896 m (19,344 ft), making it the highest point in Africa.

Mt Fuji is the highest peak in Japan at 3,776 m (12,388 ft).

Mt Vesuvius, in Italy, is 1,277 m (4,190 ft) high.

Mt Aconcagua, in the Andes, is the highest mountain in the Americas at 6,960 m (22,834 ft).

Everest dwarfs volcanoes

Even the highest volcanoes, such as Mt Kilimanjaro, fall short of Mt Everest. Size is relative, however – although Kilimanjaro is 2,952 m (9,685 ft) shorter than Everest, Kilimanjaro is still 40 times higher than the Great Pyramid, in Egypt.

Mt Elbrus, Russia: 5,642 m (18,510 ft)

Sunken volcano

Mauna Kea   Mt Everest

Mauna Kea is a volcano in Hawaii. Its base is on the seabed. Measured from there, rather than from sea level, it is 1,355 m (4,446 ft) taller than Mt Everest.

Mt Cook is New Zealand's highest peak at 3,754 m (12,316 ft).

Helen blows her top

Mt St Helen's, a volcano in Washington state, in the USA, erupted in 1980, throwing huge clouds of ash high into the sky. The ash devastated about 550 sq km (210 sq miles), an area the size of more than 2,100 tennis courts. Before the eruption the volcano was some 2,950 m (9,678 ft) high; afterwards it was about 400 m (1,310 ft) shorter.

Conifer treeline: 2,500 m (8,202 ft)

Broadleaf treeline: 1,200 m (3,937 ft)

Mt St Helen's: 2,550 m (8,366 ft)

Mt Everest:
8,848 m
(29,028 ft)

Martian mammoth

The highest volcano in the Solar System
is Olympus Mons, on Mars. It is three
times higher than Mt Everest, and
nine times higher than
Mt Olympus, in Greece.
It is thought to be
extinct.

Olympus Mons is
about 26,400 m
(86,614 ft) high.

Mt Everest

Yaks can live at heights of
more than 6,000 m (19,685 ft).

Edmund Hillary and Sherpa
Tenzing, the first people to
climb Mt Everest, pitched
their base camp at 5,486 m
(18,000 ft).

Mt McKinley, in the
Alaska Range, is the
highest mountain in
the USA at 6,194 m
(20,320 ft).

Vinson Massif, Antarctica:
5,140 m (16,864 ft)

The air at altitude

The higher you climb, the colder the air
becomes – the temperature falls about 6°C
(11°F) every 1,000 m (3,281 ft). Climbers
wear special clothing to keep warm. The
air also becomes thinner. This means there
is less oxygen in each lungful of air.
Climbers either allow time for their bodies
to adapt, or take extra oxygen supplies.

*I'm level with Hillary
and Tenzing's base
camp on Everest. Even
here the air is twice as
thin as at sea level, and
it's hard to breathe.*

The Matterhorn, in
the European Alps,
is 4,478 m (14,691 ft)
above sea level.

Mont Blanc, in the
European Alps:
4,807 m (15,770 ft)

Toverkop,
in South
Africa, rises
to 2,330 m
(7,644 ft).

Tall buildings (see pages 48-49), at the same scale as the mountains. Even
Toverkop is nearly four times as tall as the world's tallest artificial structure,
the 629-m (2,063-ft) KTHI-TV mast, in North Dakota, USA.

9,000 m
(29,528 ft)

8,000 m
(26,247 ft)

7,000 m
(22,966 ft)

6,000 m
(19,685 ft)

5,000 m
(16,404 ft)

4,000 m
(13,123 ft)

3,000 m
(9,843 ft)

2,000 m
(6,562 ft)

1,000 m
(3,281 ft)

0

GREAT LENGTHS

"IT'S HUGE! COLOSSAL! GINORMOUS!" How do you describe something so huge that it makes you dizzy just to look at it? Countless words have been written about the world's great natural wonders, but nothing can prepare you for the awe-inspiring experience of seeing them for the first time. No structures built by us humans can match nature's greatest marvels, but some of them are still pretty impressive – for example, you could drive around the USA at top speed night and day for four years and still not cover every stretch of road.

Bumble Bee Two – world's smallest biplane: wingspan 1.68 m (5 ft 6 in)

Baby Bird – world's smallest monoplane: wingspan 1.91 m (6 ft 3 in)

Albatross: wingspan 3.7 m (12 ft)

Marabou stork: wingspan 4 m (13 ft)

Silver Bullet – world's smallest jet plane: wingspan 5.2 m (17 ft)

Winged wonders of the world

A biplane (double-winged plane) called *Bumble Bee Two*, built in the 1980s by Robert H. Starr of Arizona, had a wingspan no wider than the outstretched arms of its pilot. At the other extreme, you could park 50 cars side by side on the wings of *Spruce Goose*, a flying-boat built in the USA in the 1940s by Howard Hughes, an eccentric billionaire. *Spruce Goose* barely made it into the air on its maiden flight, and covered a distance less than 10 times its own wingspan. It has not flown since and is now on display at a museum (a very big one).

USA – road network: 6,283,868 km (3,904,721 miles)

India – road network: 1,970,000 km (1,224,135 miles)

Brazil – road network: 1,670,148 km (1,037,810 miles)

USA – rail network: 240,000 km (149,133 miles)

Russia – rail network: 158,100 km (98,241 miles)

Canada – rail network: 146,444 km (90,999 miles)

China – waterways: 138,600 km (86,124 miles)

Russia – waterways: 100,000 km (62,139 miles)

Brazil – waterways: 50,000 km (31,069 miles)

On the road

The webs of roads and railways that criss-cross the globe are perhaps the biggest objects ever built. The road network of the USA tops the league – you could drive around the USA at 161 kph (100 mph), the top speed of a family car, non-stop for four years and still not cover every stretch of road. You would pass plenty of other cars, though: there are more than 141,000,000 cars in the USA – one for every 44 m (144 ft) of road.

All around the world – and the Sun

The rail network of the USA could go around the Earth's equator almost six times – yet it is tiny compared with the USA's road network. This is so vast that it could go all the way around the Sun's equator – then part of the way around again (although you would need heatproof tyres and a strong nerve to brave the melting tarmac).

The Earth's equator: 40,075 km (24,902 miles)

The 240,000-km (149,133-mile) rail network of the USA could go almost six times around the equator of the Earth. By comparison, the world's shortest rail network goes almost nowhere – Vatican City, the world's smallest state, has just 850 m (2,789 ft) of track.

USA – rail network: 240,000 km (149,133 miles)

The Earth's equator: 40,075 km (24,902 miles)

Martian metro

The world's largest metropolitan railway has enough track to cover the length of the base of the biggest mountain in the Solar System.

Olympus Mons, Mars: 600 km (373 miles) from end to end

Metropolitan railway system, Tokyo, Japan: 629 km (391 miles)

The Grand Canyon averages 1.6 km (1 mile) deep and is 446 km (277 miles) long. Eroding a layer of rock the thickness of a credit card every five years, it took the Colorado River about 10,000,000 years to excavate the gorge – an astonishingly short time in geological terms.

Sliding slowly towards the sea, the Lambert-Fischer Glacier, Antarctica, is 515 km (320 miles) long.

The Mammoth Cave system, the world's most extensive, is 567 km (352 miles) long and riddles Kentucky with holes, like a Swiss cheese.

Naturally very long

The longest of the Earth's natural features – the great rivers and mountain ranges – are truly colossal. The longest of all stretches almost from pole to pole, but is entirely hidden from sight – it is the Mid-Atlantic Ridge, a huge underwater mountain range running the full length of the Atlantic Ocean.

Made of coral and home to a huge variety of fish and other marine animals, the Great Barrier Reef stretches for 2,028 km (1,260 miles) along the coast of Queensland, Australia.

The Himalayas, Karakorams, and Hindu Kush together form an unbroken mountain range that is 3,862 km (2,400 miles) long.

The Mekong River winds 4,350 km (2,703 miles) through China, Laos, Thailand, Cambodia, and Vietnam before flowing into the South China Sea.

The Chiang Jiang River, in China, is 6,300 km (3,915 miles) long and carries half the country's riverboat traffic.

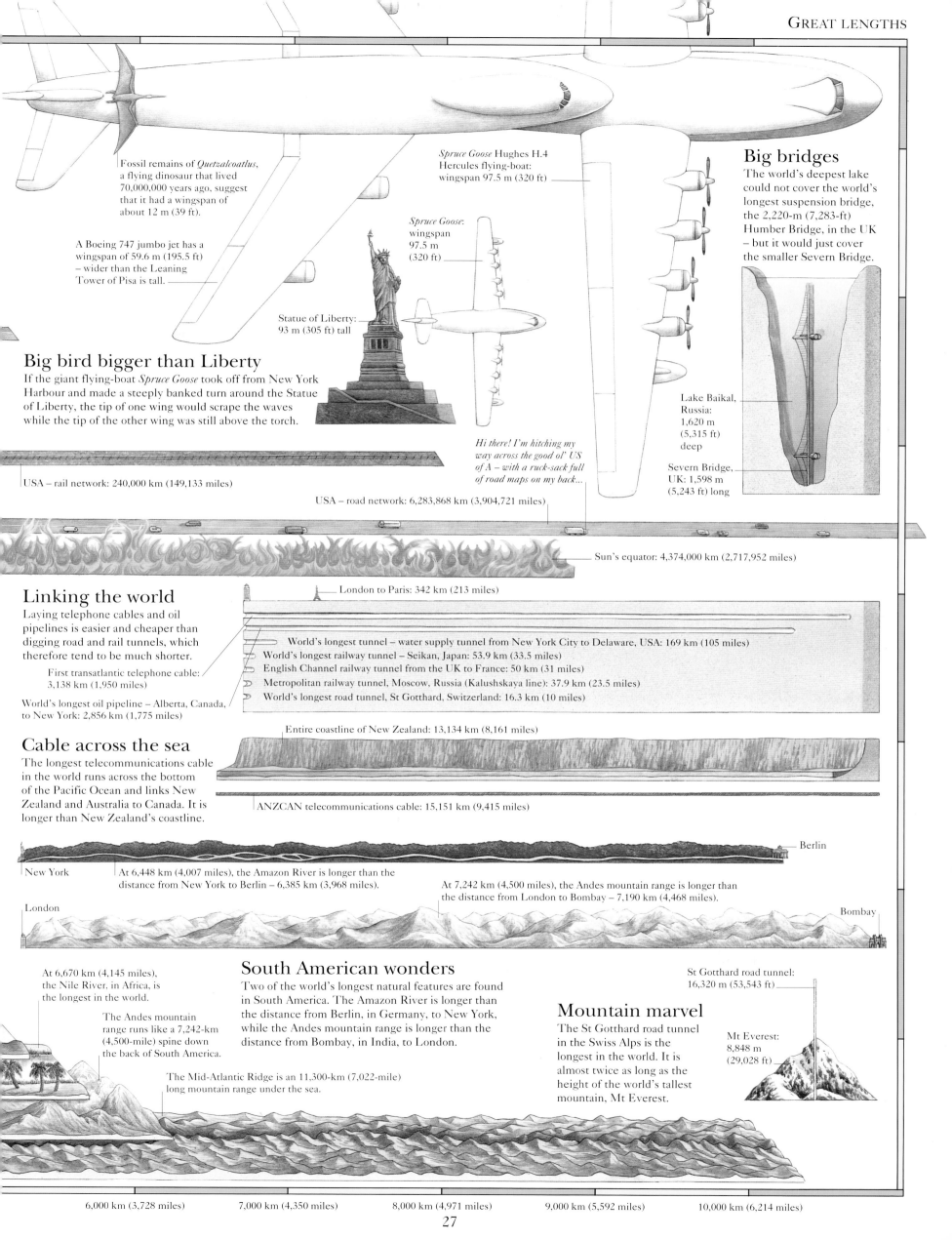

Fossil remains of *Quetzalcoatlus*, a flying dinosaur that lived 70,000,000 years ago, suggest that it had a wingspan of about 12 m (39 ft).

Spruce Goose Hughes H.4 Hercules flying-boat: wingspan 97.5 m (320 ft)

Big bridges
The world's deepest lake could not cover the world's longest suspension bridge, the 2,220-m (7,283-ft) Humber Bridge, in the UK – but it would just cover the smaller Severn Bridge.

A Boeing 747 jumbo jet has a wingspan of 59.6 m (195.5 ft) – wider than the Leaning Tower of Pisa is tall.

Spruce Goose: wingspan 97.5 m (320 ft)

Statue of Liberty: 93 m (305 ft) tall

Big bird bigger than Liberty
If the giant flying-boat *Spruce Goose* took off from New York Harbour and made a steeply banked turn around the Statue of Liberty, the tip of one wing would scrape the waves while the tip of the other wing was still above the torch.

Lake Baikal, Russia: 1,620 m (5,315 ft) deep

Severn Bridge, UK: 1,598 m (5,243 ft) long

Hi there! I'm hitching my way across the good ol' US of A – with a ruck-sack full of road maps on my back...

USA – rail network: 240,000 km (149,133 miles)

USA – road network: 6,283,868 km (3,904,721 miles)

Sun's equator: 4,374,000 km (2,717,952 miles)

Linking the world
Laying telephone cables and oil pipelines is easier and cheaper than digging road and rail tunnels, which therefore tend to be much shorter.

London to Paris: 342 km (213 miles)

World's longest tunnel – water supply tunnel from New York City to Delaware, USA: 169 km (105 miles)
World's longest railway tunnel – Seikan, Japan: 53.9 km (33.5 miles)
English Channel railway tunnel from the UK to France: 50 km (31 miles)
Metropolitan railway tunnel, Moscow, Russia (Kalushskaya line): 37.9 km (23.5 miles)
World's longest road tunnel, St Gotthard, Switzerland: 16.3 km (10 miles)

First transatlantic telephone cable: 3,138 km (1,950 miles)

World's longest oil pipeline – Alberta, Canada, to New York: 2,856 km (1,775 miles)

Entire coastline of New Zealand: 13,134 km (8,161 miles)

Cable across the sea
The longest telecommunications cable in the world runs across the bottom of the Pacific Ocean and links New Zealand and Australia to Canada. It is longer than New Zealand's coastline.

ANZCAN telecommunications cable: 15,151 km (9,415 miles)

Berlin

New York

At 6,448 km (4,007 miles), the Amazon River is longer than the distance from New York to Berlin – 6,385 km (3,968 miles).

At 7,242 km (4,500 miles), the Andes mountain range is longer than the distance from London to Bombay – 7,190 km (4,468 miles).

London

Bombay

At 6,670 km (4,145 miles), the Nile River, in Africa, is the longest in the world.

The Andes mountain range runs like a 7,242-km (4,500-mile) spine down the back of South America.

South American wonders
Two of the world's longest natural features are found in South America. The Amazon River is longer than the distance from Berlin, in Germany, to New York, while the Andes mountain range is longer than the distance from Bombay, in India, to London.

The Mid-Atlantic Ridge is an 11,300-km (7,022-mile) long mountain range under the sea.

St Gotthard road tunnel: 16,320 m (53,543 ft)

Mountain marvel
The St Gotthard road tunnel in the Swiss Alps is the longest in the world. It is almost twice as long as the height of the world's tallest mountain, Mt Everest.

Mt Everest: 8,848 m (29,028 ft)

6,000 km (3,728 miles)   7,000 km (4,350 miles)   8,000 km (4,971 miles)   9,000 km (5,592 miles)   10,000 km (6,214 miles)

WEATHER

WEATHER AFFECTS ALL of our lives, but to a greater or lesser degree depending on where we live. Some parts of the world are safe and fertile places, with comfortable amounts of sunshine, rain, and snow. Others are hot, inhospitable deserts, or frozen Arctic wastes. Then there are the hot and humid tropics – highly fertile lands, but frequently ravaged by mighty storms and floods.

Hurricane force

In summer, islands and coastal countries in the tropics are sometimes hit by severe storms, known as hurricanes in the Gulf of Mexico and Caribbean, cyclones in the Indian Ocean, and typhoons in the north-west Pacific. They can last 10 days or more, with winds of 161 kph (100 mph) – the top speed of a family car. Remarkably, the centre, or eye, of a tropical storm is calm.

Typhoons covering an area larger than that of Bangladesh – 143,998 sq km (55,600 sq miles) – frequently sweep across this country, causing widespread flooding and destruction.

When Hurricane Camille hit the coast of Mississippi and Alabama in the USA in 1969, gusts of 322 kph (200 mph) were recorded – faster than the fastest motorcycle.

Twisting tornadoes

A tornado, or twister, is a rapidly spinning column of air that whirls dust and debris high into the sky and can destroy buildings. Tornadoes at sea are called waterspouts – although short-lived, they can whisk a column of water up to cloud level.

A tornado whirling at 450 kph (280 mph) – faster than Donald Campbell's record-breaking 1964 *Bluebird* speedboat, and nearly as fast as a drag car – struck Wichita Falls, in Texas, in the USA, in 1958.

The Empire State Building is 381 m (1,250 ft) high. A waterspout four times as high, at 1,528 m (5,014 ft), was seen off Australia in 1898.

Bluebird speedboat: 445 kph (277 mph)

Drag car: 497 kph (309 mph)

Continental extremes

A comparison of the greatest extremes of temperature – the hottest and coldest on record for each continent – shows that Oceania has the smallest range and Asia the greatest.

MAXIMUM TEMPERATURE

Oceania: 53°C (127°F)

South America: 49°C (120°F)

Africa: 58°C (136°F)

Antarctica: 14°C (57°F)

Europe: 50°C (122°F)

North America: 57°C (135°F)

Asia: 54°C (129°F)

MINIMUM TEMPERATURE

Oceania: –22°C (–8°F)

South America: –33°C (–27°F)

Africa: –24°C (–11°F)

Antarctica: –89°C (–128°F)

Europe: –55°C (–67°F)

North America: –63°C (–81°F)

Asia: –68°C (–90°F)

The wind and the water

The Beaufort scale of wind speeds is used worldwide in weather reports and forecasts compiled for ships and boats at sea. It was invented in 1805 by British Admiral Sir Francis Beaufort. The scale ranges from Force 0, representing a calm sea, through Force 8, representing a gale, to Force 12 and above, signifying hurricane-strength winds.

0 – calm: 0-2 kph (0-1 mph)
1 – light air: 2-5 kph (1-3 mph)
2 – light breeze: 6-11 kph (4-7 mph)
3 – gentle breeze: 12-19 kph (8-12 mph)
4 – moderate breeze: 20-29 kph (12-18 mph)
5 – fresh breeze: 30-38 kph (19-24 mph)
6 – strong breeze: 39-50 kph (24-31 mph)
7 – high wind: 51-61 kph (32-38 mph)
8 – gale: 62-74 kph (38-46 mph)

Fire and ice

Between the fiery surface of the Sun and the absolute cold of space there is only a narrow band of temperatures where life is possible. Even within this narrow band there are huge variations, however – from the searing heat of some deserts to the icy polar wastes.

The surface of the Sun is a scorching 5,330°C (9,626°F).

At sea level, fresh water boils at 100°C (212°F).

The temperature at the bottom of the world's deepest mines reaches 73°C (163°F).

The highest temperature ever recorded in the shade – 57.8°C (136°F), at al'Aziziyah, in the Libyan desert, in September 1922 – was hot enough to fry an egg.

Cloncurry, Australia, has recorded temperatures as high as 52.8°C (127°F).

The top summer temperature in Rome, Italy, is a hot but tolerable 40°C (104°F).

Over the period 1960-66 an average temperature of 34.4°C (94°F) was recorded for Dallol, in Ethiopia – the hottest on Earth.

Fresh water freezes at 0°C (32°F) at sea level.

A comfortable room temperature is considered to be 20°C (68°F).

That's much better!

100°C (212°F)	90°C (194°F)	80°C (176°F)	70°C (158°F)	60°C (140°F)	50°C (122°F)	40°C (104°F)	30°C (86°F)	20°C (68°F)	10°C (50°F)

Clouds in the sky

The lowest clouds, stratus, form below 460 m (1,509 ft) – not much higher than the world's tallest office building, the 443-m (1,453-ft) high Sears Tower, in Chicago, Illinois, in the USA. The highest clouds, cirrus, can be seen at 13,700 m (44,948 ft) – nearly 5,000 m (16,404 ft) higher than the world's highest mountain.

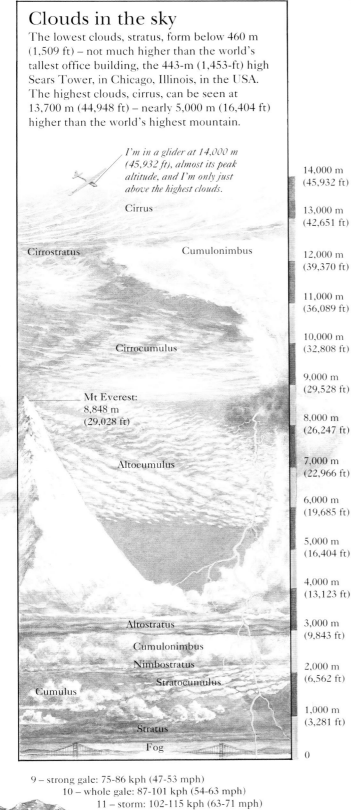

I'm in a glider at 14,000 m (45,932 ft), almost its peak altitude, and I'm only just above the highest clouds.

Cirrus

Cirrostratus

Cumulonimbus

Cirrocumulus

Mt Everest: 8,848 m (29,028 ft)

Altocumulus

Altostratus

Cumulonimbus

Nimbostratus

Stratocumulus

Cumulus

Stratus

Fog

14,000 m (45,932 ft)

13,000 m (42,651 ft)

12,000 m (39,370 ft)

11,000 m (36,089 ft)

10,000 m (32,808 ft)

9,000 m (29,528 ft)

8,000 m (26,247 ft)

7,000 m (22,966 ft)

6,000 m (19,685 ft)

5,000 m (16,404 ft)

4,000 m (13,123 ft)

3,000 m (9,843 ft)

2,000 m (6,562 ft)

1,000 m (3,281 ft)

0

Lightning strikes

The Earth is struck by lightning 100 times a second. High-speed photography shows that each strike consists of a lead stroke and a return stroke. The lead stroke travels at 160-1,600 km (99-994 miles) per second and forks as it opens a channel from the clouds to the ground. The much brighter return stroke flashes up this channel at about 140,000 km (86,994 miles) per second, or nearly half the speed of light.

Lightning can extend up to 32 km (20 miles). A space shuttle takes only 100 seconds to travel this high from lift-off, but the return stroke of a lightning bolt is more than 400,000 times as fast.

A typical lightning bolt is about 800 m (2,625 ft) long – almost three times the height of the Eiffel Tower, which is 321 m (1,052 ft).

Tenpin hailstones

On 3 September 1970, hailstones up to 760 g (1 lb 11 oz) in weight and up to 20 cm (8 in) in diameter – as big as tenpin bowling balls – fell at Coffeyville, Kansas, in the USA.

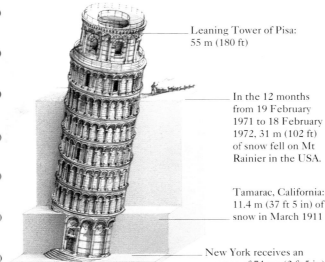

Leaning Tower of Pisa: 55 m (180 ft)

In the 12 months from 19 February 1971 to 18 February 1972, 31 m (102 ft) of snow fell on Mt Rainier in the USA.

Tamarac, California: 11.4 m (37 ft 5 in) of snow in March 1911

New York receives an average of 74 cm (2 ft 5 in) of snow every year.

Snowed under

There are records of nearly 2 m (6.5 ft) of snow falling in one day – enough to bury a standing adult. Single snowstorms have resulted in falls of almost 5 m (16 ft) – enough to cover three adults standing on each other's shoulders. In 12 months, enough snow falls on the world's snowiest place, Mt Rainier, in Washington state, in the USA, to bury more than half of the Leaning Tower of Pisa.

Rain around the world

Annual rainfall varies greatly worldwide. Aswan, Egypt, has a measly 0.5 mm (0.02 in). However, Bonaventura, Colombia, has a drenching 6.7 m (22 ft) – enough to cover almost four adults standing on each other's shoulders. Meanwhile, at Mt Waialeale, Hawaii, it rains on up to 350 days every year.

Cilaos, La Réunion, Indian Ocean, 15-16 March 1952 – highest ever rainfall in 24 hours: 1.87 m (6 ft 2 in)

Madrid, Spain: average annual rainfall 42 cm (16.5 in)

Cherrapunji, Assam, India, 1 August 1860-31 July 1861 – highest annual total rainfall : 26.5 m (87 ft)

9 – strong gale: 75-86 kph (47-53 mph)
10 – whole gale: 87-101 kph (54-63 mph)
11 – storm: 102-115 kph (63-71 mph)

8 9

10

11   12

12 – hurricane: 116-132 kph (72-82 mph)
13 – hurricane: 133-149 kph (83-93 mph)
14 – hurricane: 150-166 kph (93-103 mph)

13

14   15

15-17: hurricanes of 166-218 kph (103-135 mph)... rarely encountered, but cause massive destruction

16

17

Norilsk, Russia, is the coldest inhabited place in the world, with an average temperature of −10.9°C (12.4°F).

At an average −57.8°C (−72°F), Polus Nedostupnosti, in Antarctica, is the coldest place on Earth.

The coldest temperature ever recorded on the surface of the Earth was −89.2°C (−128.6°F), at Vostok, Antarctica, in 1983.

Temperatures in outer space plunge to within 3°C (4°F) of the coldest temperature possible, known as absolute zero: −273.16°C (−459.69°F).

The lowest temperature ever recorded in the upper atmosphere was −143°C (−225°F), 80 km (50 miles) above Kronogard, Sweden, in 1963.

−20°C (−4°F)	−40°C (−40°F)	−60°C (−76°F)	−80°C (−112°F)	−100°C (−148°F)	−120°C (−184°F)	−140°C (−220°F)	−160°C (−292°F)	−180°C (−184°F)	−200°C (−328°F)	−220°C (−364°F)	−240°C (−400°F)	−260°C (−436°F)

DISASTERS

"STOP PRESS – HUNDREDS DIE in earthquake!" "Famine tragedy – thousands starve."
Newspaper headlines and television news flashes like these make us feel mixed emotions:
shock at first, then sympathy as we watch rescue workers and helpers – perhaps even
excitement when we read about lucky escapes. We also feel relieved that we are not
among the victims, especially when the disaster happens close to home. It is easy to think,
"It could have been me." Disasters on the other side of the world have much less impact
on us, even when they are far more catastrophic.

Oiling the waters

Worldwide, modern tankers safely carry 60 bathtubs of crude oil for every teaspoonful accidentally spilled.

Some 350,000,000 litres (76,990,761 gallons) of crude oil spilled into the Carribean when the tankers *Atlantic Empress* and *Aegean Captain* collided off Trinidad & Tobago in 1979.

In 1978 the tanker *Amoco Cadiz* spilled 268,000,000 litres (58,952,925 gallons) of crude oil into the sea off the coast of France.

The largest oil tankers – supertankers – can carry as much as 650,000,000 litres (142,982,840 gallons) of crude oil at a time. That is about 4.5 litres (1 gallon) for every car in the USA, so a major spill can spread over a vast area of the sea and pollute a huge length of coastline. However, nothing can ever protect the oceans against deliberate releases of oil such as the one by Iraq in 1991,during the Gulf War.

The explosive eruption of the volcanic island of Krakatoa triggered a 37-m (120-ft) high tsunami, or giant ocean wave.

In 1991 Iraq deliberately discharged 1,713,000,000 litres (376,814,780 gallons) of crude oil into the Persian Gulf.

When the *Torrey Canyon* ran aground off the coast of Great Britain in 1967 it spilled 139,000,000 litres (30,576,330 gallons) of crude oil into the sea.

In 1989 the *Exxon Valdez* spilled 41,000,000 litres (9,018,918 gallons) of crude oil into the sea off the coast of Alaska.

Ships left high and dry

The Aral Sea, in Kazakhstan and Uzbekistan, was once the world's fourth biggest lake. Until the 1960s, 56 cubic km (13 cubic miles) of water flowed into it each year. Since the 1960s, 97 per cent of this water has been diverted for irrigation and industry. As a result, the Aral Sea is steadily drying up. An area the size of Lake Tanganyika, in Africa, has already been lost. The lake now covers about half its original area – with ships left rusting away on dry land, and the lake nowhere in sight.

Aral Sea in 1964: about 65,500 sq km (25,292 sq miles)

Aral Sea in 1993: about 36,500 sq km (14,094 sq miles)

Krakatoa catastrophe

In 1883 a series of huge blasts blew apart the volcanic island of Krakatoa, in Indonesia, killing 36,000 people. Heard some 4,800 km (2,983 miles) away, the blasts ejected 21 cubic km (5 cubic miles) of dust into the air – more than 8,000 times the volume of the Great Pyramid.

Sea takes greatest toll

Most of the worst transport disasters are at sea, but since long-distance travellers switched to flying, plane crashes have grabbed the headlines. This makes some people afraid of flying, when in fact it is one of the safest forms of travel.

Challenger space shuttle, USA, 1986: seven die in explosion shortly after take-off

Hindenburg airship, New Jersey, USA, 1937: 36 die in mooring explosion

Le Mans motor racing circuit, France, 1955: 82 die when car crashes and explodes

New York Subway, 1918: 97 die in train crash

Air India 747, Irish Sea, 1985: 329 die in mid-air aircraft explosion

Japan Air Lines 747, Japan, 1985: 520 die in mountain plane crash

KLM & Pan Am 747s, Canary Islands, 1977: 583 die in airport runway collision

Railway, Bihar, India, 1981: 800 die when train plunges off bridge

Titanic passenger liner, North Atlantic, 1912: 1,517 die in sinking of ship after it hits iceberg

Sultana steamboat, Mississippi, 1865: 1,547 die in river boat explosion

Salang Tunnel (road and rail), Afghanistan, 1982: 3,000 die in petrol tanker crash and explosion

Donna Paz ferry, Philippines, 1987: 3,000 die when oil tanker rams ferry

The biggest killers

Disease and famine kill far more people than wars or natural disasters. The Black Death killed up to three-quarters of all people in Europe in the 14th century. Without modern drugs, a similar plague today could kill 4,000,000,000 people.

Rat fleas spread the plague when they bite people.

Malaria, spread by mosquito bites in the tropics: worldwide, 2,000,000 die each year

Korean War, 1950-53: 1,900,000 die in battle

Irish potato famine, 1846-51: 1,500,000 die

Bangladesh cyclone, 1970: 1,000,000 die

Black Death: 75,000,000 die

Famine, China, 1959-61: 30,000,000 die

Influenza, worldwide, 1918: 21,600,000 die

World War II, 1939-45: 16,000,000 die in battle

World War I, 1914-18: 8,500,000 die in battle

Explosive force

Some modern nuclear warheads are 1,250 times as powerful as the atomic bomb dropped on Hiroshima. But the Tunguska explosion was 1,500 times as powerful as the Hiroshima bomb, while the combined force of the four Krakatoa explosions was 10,000 times more powerful.

Hiroshima bomb
Equal to 20,320 tonnes (20,000 tons) of ordinary TNT explosive

Tunguska meteorite
Equal to 30,500,000 tonnes (30,000,000 tons) of TNT

Krakatoa volcano
Equal to 203,000,000 tonnes (200,000,000 tons) of TNT

Tunguska meteorite

Lava not the real killer

Not all volcanoes kill through sudden explosions or eruptions. In 1783, Laki volcano, in Iceland, spewed out lava – molten rock – for two months. The lava filled two valleys, but killed very few people directly. Most of the 10,000 deaths were caused by sulphurous fumes, and by starvation resulting from volcanic ash killing crops and animals.

The lava was 30 m (98 ft) deep – enough to bury a 20-m (66-ft) four-storey town house.

Siberian shocker

One day in 1908 a blast filled the sky above Tunguska, in Siberia, a remote area of Russia. Heard 1,000 km (621 miles) away, it flattened trees over 5,000 sq km (1,931 sq miles), an area twice the size of Luxembourg, but no-one was killed. Scientists believe a large meteorite exploded as it hit the upper atmosphere.

Only the tip of the 553-m (1,815-ft) CN Tower, in Toronto, Canada, would clear the top of the cone.

Cone in a cornfield

The 1943 eruption of Parícutin, in Mexico, killed no-one, but as the volcano grew it engulfed a village and destroyed large areas of farmland. It appeared, almost without warning, in a cornfield.

Hiroshima

In 1945 an atomic bomb was dropped on the city of Hiroshima, in Japan. It killed about 140,000 people and almost totally destroyed the city.

Hiroshima atomic bomb

One day after the cone first appeared it was 10 m (33 ft) high.

Parícutin

Only one year after the cone first appeared it was 450 m (1,476 ft) high. At the peak of its activity it was ejecting 2,440 tonnes (2,400 tons) of material a minute. In 1952 the cone was measured at 528 m (1,732 ft).

China's flood hazard

China's Yellow River regularly floods huge areas of farmland. Heavy rains in 1887 caused it to flood an area one-and-a-half times the size of Ireland. The areas devastated by some of the world's most famous city fires are tiny by comparison.

Great Fire of London, 1666: 1.9 sq km (0.7 sq miles) destroyed

Chicago, 1871: fire destroys 8.9 sq km (3.4 sq miles)

Yellow River, 1887: 125,000 sq km (48,266 sq miles) flooded

Area of Ireland: 83,850 sq km (32,377 sq miles)

Disaster areas

Diseases, such as the plague, can cause worldwide destruction, but most disasters are far less extensive. Those that have the most widespread effects are floods, which can drown small countries. Global warming, caused by atmospheric pollution trapping the Sun's heat, could in future cause worse floods than anything yet seen, as rising sea levels wash over coastal cities.

Bad vibrations

The Richter scale of earthquake size measures how much the ground moves, but is not a guide to the destruction caused – that depends much more on the structure of the rock and earth where the earthquake strikes, and on the construction of the local buildings.

San Francisco, 1906: 8.25 on the Richter scale – about 500 die

Wilhelm Gustloff refugee ship, Baltic Sea, 1945: 7,700 die when torpedoed ship sinks – death toll equal to almost 14 full jumbo jets

Tangshan, China, 1976: 7.8 on the Richter scale 655,000 die

Kobe, Japan, 1995: 6.8 on the Richter scale 4,800 die

Mt St Helen's, 1980: ash from volcano covers 550 sq km (212 sq miles)

San Francisco, 1906: fire caused by earthquake destroys 12 sq km (4.6 sq miles)

Exxon Valdez oil spill, 1989: 1,295 sq km (500 sq miles)

Bush fires, South Australia, 1983: 5,180 sq km (2,000 sq miles)

Mississippi River, 1927: floods cover 46,600 sq km (17,994 sq miles)

5,000 people   6,000 people   7,000 people   8,000 people

GREAT AND SMALL

COULD ANTS GROW big enough to eat people? Why are the largest animals living today found in the sea, and not on land? The simple answer to such fascinating questions is that animal size is governed by nature. We need not fear the jaws of giant insects, because giant insects would soon suffocate – their simple breathing tubes could not supply them with enough air. Fierce competition for food stops the largest land animals, elephants, from being bigger. When giant dinosaurs roamed the Earth they had no competitors – but they needed legs like tree trunks to support their heavy bodies. The biggest animals today, blue whales, feed freely on almost unlimited supplies of krill, a shrimp-like creature. Whales' bodies are adapted to the buoyancy of the sea – on land, they would be crushed by their own weight.

At up to 5.8 m (19 ft), a fully grown giraffe is so tall that its arteries have special valves to help pump blood up to its head. Without these valves, its heart would have to be as big as its whole body.

Adult bull African elephants grow to more than 3 m (10 ft) tall.

Twice as tall as all the rest

The giraffe is by far the tallest animal. It is twice as tall as the African elephant, and more than three times as tall as the average man. Its long legs and long neck allow it to browse on tree-top leaves beyond the reach of even the elephant's long trunk.

Rearing on its hind legs, the grizzly bear of North America can be 3 m (10 ft) tall.

With its long legs and long neck, an ostrich can be 2.7 m (9 ft) tall.

Long gone Jurassic giant

The biggest dinosaurs were plant eaters. They were bigger than any living land animals, because they had no competitors. One of the longest, measured from nose to tip of tail, was *Diplodocus*, which lived on the North American continent some 145,000,000 years ago. *Diplodocus* was nearly three times as long as the longest land animal living today, the reticulated python.

Found in Asia, and growing up to 10.7 m (35 ft) – almost half the length of a tennis court – the reticulated python is the longest snake in the world.

The Nile crocodile grows up to 5 m (16 ft) in length – more than 125 times as long as the world's smallest gecko.

Bull African elephants can be 5 m (16 ft) long – more than 7 m (23 ft) if you include their trunks and tails.

The Giant Indian rhinoceros grows up to 4.3 m (14 ft) long – about the length of a small car.

A dromedary camel can be 3 m (10 ft) long from the end of its nose to the base of its tail.

A tiger can be 2.8 m (9 ft) long – about six times as long as a domestic cat.

At 12 m (39 ft 4 in), the rare, warm-water whale shark is about one-third as long as a blue whale. Luckily for us, it feeds on plankton and is completely harmless.

Including their tentacles, giant deep-sea squid can be up to 17.5 m (57 ft) long.

Gigantic jellyfish

In the buoyant, food-rich world of the sea, animals can grow to enormous sizes. The blue whale has the longest body, but if you include the tentacles, the Arctic giant jellyfish is the longest sea creature of all. Fanned out, its tentacles would form a circle covering an area bigger than 15 tennis courts.

The giant spider crab, found off Japan, has a body about 25 cm (10 in) in diameter but a leg span up to 3.7 m (12 ft).

10 m (33 ft)

Big eyes not always best

Giant squid have eyes as big as watermelons, but much worse eyesight than humans. Some birds of prey have smaller eyes than ours, but 10 times sharper vision.

Human eye: diameter 2.4 cm (1 in)

Golf ball: diameter 4.6 cm (1.8 in)

Horse's eye: diameter 5.5 cm (2 in)

Tennis ball: diameter 6.5 cm (2.5 in)

Giant squid's eye: diameter 38 cm (15 in)

Patu marplesi, a spider found in Western Samoa, has a leg span of only 0.43 mm (0.017 in).

Cuban arrow-poison frog (actual size): 1.2 cm (0.5 in) long

Giraffe towers over tallest people

Most people stop growing at about age 18, but some keep on growing. Before treatment for this problem was available, a few grew taller than 2.44 m (8 ft). That might seem tall, but a giraffe would still have to stoop to look them in the eye.

Although much broader, heavier, and stronger than humans, adult gorillas are not much taller, at 2 m (6.5 ft).

Worldwide, the average man is 1.75 m (5 ft 9 in) tall.

Giraffe: up to 5.8 m (19 ft) tall

Worldwide, the average height for women is 1.65 m (5 ft 5 in).

Stupendous spider

The smallest frog could sit on your thumbnail – yet dozens of the tiniest spiders could dance on its head. Were it not poisonous, however, the same frog would only be a snack for the biggest spider, which could then tackle both the smallest lizard and the smallest snake.

West Indian gecko, or lizard (actual size): less than 4 cm (1.5 in) long

Diplodocus was 23-27 m (75-89 ft) long from nose to tip of tail.

Average woman: 1.65 m (5 ft 5 in)

Average man: 1.75 m (5 ft 9 in) tall

Robert Wadlow, USA (1918-40) – world's tallest recorded man: 2.72 m (8 ft 11 in)

Dizzy big beetle

The massive armour of the Goliath beetle makes it the world's heaviest flying insect, weighing about the same as eight house mice. The size of the beetle makes it a popular pet in its native Africa, where children fly it in circles on a string, just like a control-line toy aeroplane.

South American bird-eating spider (actual size): leg span up to 28 cm (11 in)

Zebras can grow up to 2.3 m (7.5 ft) long.

The Goliath beetle can be 11 cm (4.3 in) long and weigh 100 g (3.5 oz).

A fully grown house mouse has a 6.5-cm (2.5-in) long body and weighs about 12 g (0.4 oz).

Eight house mice weigh about the same as one Goliath beetle.

Snake tops longest leap

If you laid a full-sized reticulated python out straight, it would stretch 20 per cent further than the world record long jump. (Don't choose a hungry snake, because pythons can swallow children whole.)

Reticulated python: 10.7 m (35 ft)

The world record for the long jump, set by Mike Powell of the USA, in 1991, is 8.95 m (29 ft 4.5 in).

0

11 m (36 ft)

Dimwitted dinosaur

Humans are smart, but our brains are not the biggest. A human brain is as big as a grapefruit – a sperm whale's brain is six-and-a-half times larger. Other big animals manage with tiny brains. *Stegosaurus*, a dinosaur, weighed as much as 25 men, but had a brain the size of a walnut.

The average adult human brain weighs 1.4 kg (3 lb).

Stegosaurus was 6 m (20 ft) long and weighed some 1.5 tonnes (1.5 tons), but its brain only weighed about 70 g (2.5 oz).

A fully grown sperm whale can be 20 m (66 ft) long and has a brain weighing about 9.2 kg (20.3 lb).

It's a good job blue whales don't eat people, otherwise I would be in serious trouble down here!

The rare West Indian thread snake, shown here actual size, is only about 10 cm (4 in) long – more than 100 times shorter than the reticulated python.

A blue whale can be 33.5 m (110 ft) long – about the length of 18 scuba divers, including their flippers.

The Arctic giant jellyfish can grow to more than 35 m (115 ft) long, including its stinging tentacles, which drift in the sea like a fisherman's net, ready to snare unwary small fish.

20 m (66 ft)

30 m (98 ft)

40 m (131 ft)

LIGHT AND HEAVY

SIZE AND WEIGHT do not always go hand in hand. A hummingbird and a golf ball are much the same size, but it takes as many as 28 hummingbirds to equal the weight of one golf ball. The heaviest metal, osmium, weighs more than 40 times as much as the lightest, lithium. The range of weights in both the human and natural worlds is enormous. The world's largest bell, the Tsar Kolokol bell, weighs almost as much as the Statue of Liberty, yet the statue is more than seven times as tall – while the heaviest mammal, the blue whale, can weigh an incredible 90,000,000 times more than the lightest, the pygmy shrew.

From heavy metal to lightweight lithium

The heaviest metal, and the heaviest element, is osmium. A 30-cm (12-in) cube of osmium would weigh about 610 kg (1,345 lb), or as much as 10 adults, each weighing 61 kg (134 lb). A 30-cm (12-in) cube of lithium, the lightest metal, would tip the scales at only 14.4 kg (32 lb) – not much heavier than the average two-year-old boy.

A 30-cm (12-in) cube of osmium would weigh as much as ten 61-kg (134-lb) adults.

The average two-year-old boy weighs 11.8 kg (26 lb).

A 30-cm (12-in) cube of lithium would weigh only 14.4 kg (32 lb).

Where did that rocket come from? Suddenly this tree-climbing lark doesn't seem such a good idea!

The General Sherman giant sequoia is nearly 84 m (276 ft) tall and weighs an estimated 2,500 tonnes (2,461 tons).

Large weight of living wood

The largest living thing on Earth is the General Sherman giant sequoia tree, in Sequoia National Park, California. It weighs an estimated 2,500 tonnes (2,461 tons) – almost as much as a fuel-laden *Saturn V* rocket at lift-off.

At lift-off, a *Saturn V* rocket stood 111 m (364 ft) tall and weighed more than 2,960 tonnes (2,913 tons).

Almost a rocket a storey

Built between 1929 and 1931, the rocket-shaped 102-storey concrete and steel Empire State Building weighs about the same as 112 *Saturn V* rockets at lift-off.

The Empire State Building weighs 331,122 tonnes (325,907 tons).

Altogether, 112 *Saturn V* rockets at lift-off would weigh more than 331,520 tonnes (326,299 tons).

Lighter and heavier than air

Hydrogen is the lightest gas, radon the heaviest. *Graf Zeppelin II*, one of the two largest airships ever built, held almost 200,000 cubic m (7,062,895 cubic ft) of hydrogen, weighing little more than three bull African elephants. Filled with radon, it could not have flown – the gas would have weighed as much as 400 elephants.

All the hydrogen in *Graf Zeppelin II* weighed less than 18 tonnes (18 tons).

An adult bull African elephant weighs about 5 tonnes (5 tons).

Graf Zeppelin II was about 245 m (804 ft) long.

Had *Graf Zeppelin II* been filled with radon, the gas would have weighed more than 2,000 tonnes (1,969 tons) – as much as 400 bull African elephants.

A whale of a rocket

A *Saturn V* rocket at lift-off weighed about the same as 23 fully grown blue whales. Most of the weight was accounted for by three full fuel tanks and three sets of engines, which were fired and jettisoned in succession.

Adult blue whales weigh about 130 tonnes (128 tons) each – so 23 adult blue whales weigh about 2,990 tonnes (2,943 tons).

Saturn V rocket: more than 2,960 tonnes (2,913 tons)

Tower's iron tonnage

Modifications to the Eiffel Tower steadily increased its weight from about 9,700 tonnes (9,547 tons) when it was completed in 1889, but in 1983 it was reduced to its present 8,757 tonnes (8,619 tons) – almost three times the weight of a *Saturn V* rocket at lift-off.

Made of iron, the Eiffel Tower weighs 8,757 tonnes (8,619 tons). Every seven years it is repainted with 5 tonnes (5 tons) of paint.

Three *Saturn V* rockets at lift-off would weigh more than 8,880 tonnes (8,740 tons).

Twenty-eight bee hummingbirds

=

One 45-g (1.6-oz) golf ball

Small for their size...

A bee hummingbird, the world's smallest bird, weighs only about 1.6 g (0.06 oz), while a pygmy shrew, the world's smallest mammal, weighs only about 1.5 g (0.05 oz). Both are about the size of a golf ball, but one 45-g (1.6-oz) golf ball weighs as much as 28 bee hummingbirds or 30 pygmy shrews.

Thirty pygmy shrews

=

One 45-g (1.6-oz) golf ball

Mammoth mammals

Blue whales are the largest animals on Earth. Nobody has ever managed to weigh one intact, but they grow to an estimated 130 tonnes (128 tons) – about 26 times as heavy as a bull African elephant, the largest animal on land. In turn, a bull African elephant is about 26 times heavier than the average pig. Like pygmy shrews, blue whales are mammals – but they can be an incredible 90,000,000 times as heavy.

The average pig weighs 192 kg (423 lb). A bull African elephant weighs some 5 tonnes (5 tons) – about the same as 26 pigs.

One 130-tonne (128-ton) blue whale weighs about the same as 26 bull African elephants.

Jumbo flying bird

The ostrich is the biggest bird on Earth but, although it can run fast, it is unable to fly. The heaviest bird that can fly is the great bustard, which can weigh as much as the average six-year-old boy – and more than 13,000 times as much as a bee hummingbird.

The average six-year-old boy weighs 20.9 kg (46 lb).

A fully grown great bustard can also weigh 20.9 kg (46 lb).

Lightweight Liberty

Excluding the pedestal, the Statue of Liberty is surprisingly light – only about one-and-a-half times the weight of a fully grown blue whale. It weighs much less than you might expect because, rather than being solid, it is a thin layer of copper over an iron framework.

The Statue of Liberty weighs only 204 tonnes (201 tons).

A fully grown blue whale weighs about 130 tonnes (128 tons).

Worth its weight...

Throughout human history, gold has been coveted and valued for its beauty and rarity. Gold is also one of the heaviest of all metals. It is estimated that all the gold ever mined would weigh a total of about 150,000 tonnes (147,638 tons). That sounds like a lot, but in fact it would only make a solid block about the size of a tennis court.

A tennis court is 23.8 m (78 ft) long and 11 m (36 ft) wide.

All the gold ever mined would make a cube with 19.8-m (65-ft) sides.

Big bronze bell

The world's largest bell is the Tsar Kolokol bell at the Kremlin, in Moscow, Russia. Cast from bronze in 1735, it cracked, and has never been rung. Amazingly, it is almost as heavy as the much bigger Statue of Liberty.

Excluding the pedestal, the Statue of Liberty is 46 m (151 ft) high and weighs 204 tonnes (201 tons).

The Tsar Kolokol bell is 6.14 m (20 ft) high and weighs 201.9 tonnes (199 tons).

Person drawn to scale

Solid as a rock

Made from more than 2,000,000 blocks of limestone, the Great Pyramid weighs almost 16 times as much as the Empire State Building – which, remarkably, weighs less than the 17-m (56-ft) depth of earth that was excavated for its foundations.

One Empire State Building weighs 331,122 tonnes (325,907 tons) – so 16 of them would weigh 5,297,952 tonnes (5,214,520 tons).

The Great Pyramid weighs an estimated 5,216,400 tonnes (5,134,252 tons).

ANIMAL SPEED

SOME ANIMALS ARE CAPABLE of great speed, which they use to chase prey or to escape from predators. Other animals live much more leisurely lives. From the proverbial slowness of the snail to the legendary swiftness of the cheetah – more than 2,000 times as fast – the range of speeds found in the animal world is astonishing. Recording them is not easy, however. Measuring how fast an animal can swim or fly is especially tricky. It is also important not to mistake a sudden spurt for an animal's normal top speed.

Micro movers

The speed of microscopic creatures is expressed in micrometres (millionths of a metre) a second.

Bacteria: up to 100 micrometres a second

Common snail: 0.05 kph (0.03 mph)

Sloth: 0.19 kph (0.12 mph)

Snail's pace

Even at its fastest, the common snail is 100 times slower than a child's normal walking speed.

FLYING THROUGH THE AIR

Birds were the world's fastest creatures until diving World War I aircraft began to exceed even the speed of a diving peregrine falcon, which can touch 350 kph (217 mph). With the aid of wind and gravity, even very small birds can manage 97 kph (60 mph).

Dragonfly: 29 kph (18 mph)

Darting by

Dragonflies are the fastest insects in the world, flying at up to 29 kph (18 mph) – maybe even faster.

As the crow flies

Crows and other common birds average speeds of 32-48 kph (20-30 mph).

Crow: 32-48 kph (20-30 mph)

Guano bat: 51 kph (32 mph)

Batmobility

Active only at night, the speedy guano bat uses sonar to stop it flying into things in the dark.

CHAMPION RUNNERS

Some land animals, such as cheetahs, are sprinters, capable of sudden but short bursts of speed. Others, like elephants, are slower, but can maintain a steady pace for longer.

Heavy going

Despite its great bulk, a charging African elephant can hit 40 kph (25 mph), easily outrunning a human athlete.

If cheetahs had to go to school every day, I bet they would be even slower than me!

African elephant: 40 kph (25 mph)

Fast track

Humans can run a long way at a steady pace, but can only sprint in short bursts. The men's world 100 m record is just under 10 seconds.

First steps

A child's normal walking speed – except on the way to school – is just under 5 kph (3 mph).

Child walking: a little less than 5 kph (3 mph)

Female sprinter: 34 kph (21 mph)

Male sprinter: 36 kph (22 mph)

Cat: 48 kph (30 mph)

Rocketing ratcatchers

Cats can accelerate to 48 kph (30 mph) – which is bad luck for rats, whose top speed is less than 10 kph (6 mph).

SWIM KINGS RULE THE WAVES

The fastest fish and mammals in the sea are generally those with long bodies and powerful tails. Although they rarely exceed 10 times their own body length per second, and the endurance of many is limited, some species are awesome performers in the water.

Dolphin: 48 kph (30 mph)

In the swim

Dolphins can swim at 48 kph (30 mph), and maintain this speed over long distances.

Male swimmer: 8 kph (5 mph)

Gentoo penguin: 35 kph (22 mph)

Penguin power

The gentoo penguin of the Antarctic is thought to be the fastest swimming bird in the world.

At full stretch

Compared with many animals, human swimmers are slowcoaches in the water, with 8 kph (5 mph) the apparent limit for a male Olympic freestyle swimmer.

Sea trout: 24 kph (15 mph)

Quick fish

Sea trout can swim five times as fast as a child can walk.

Tiger shark: 53 kph (33 mph)

Go-faster shark

Tiger sharks can swim six times faster than the fastest humans.

0 | 10 kph (6 mph) | 20 kph (12 mph) | 25 kph (16 mph) | 35 kph (22 mph) | 45 kph (28 mph) | 50 kph (31 mph)

FASTER AND FASTER

RACING A POWERBOAT, driving a fast car, flying a jet – all provide a thrilling dose of speed. In the excitement it is easy to forget that speed is a modern experience. Our ancestors went no faster than they could ride on horseback. For most people the first taste of speed came with the railways. Flight brought even greater speeds, but not right away. When humans first flew, in 1903, the fastest train could do 210 kph (130 mph), a speed that aircraft did not reach for another 15 years. Space flight is the ultimate thrill. Plummeting back to Earth, the *Apollo 10* astronauts travelled as far in three seconds as they could run in three hours. Space travel is not yet available to all, but long-distance travel on Earth, by land, sea, or air, is now commonplace.

Hopping into the history books

The first powered flight was made in the USA, in 1903, by Orville Wright, and lasted an estimated 12 seconds. We will never know exactly how long Orville was airborne, because his brother Wilbur was so excited that he forgot to stop his stop-watch. The brothers did measure the distance of the flight – at 37 m (120 ft), it was less than the wingspan of a jumbo jet.

In August 1960 Joseph Kittinger stepped out of a balloon 31,330 m (102,789 ft) above Tularosa, in New Mexico, in the USA.

Speedy sky-divers

Before pulling their rip-cords, sport parachutists relish a few moments of breathtaking speed in free-fall. They accelerate until air resistance stops them from falling faster. Depending on their size, clothing, and posture, they can reach about 195 kph (121 mph). However, plunging from a balloon at 31,330 m (102,789 ft), in 1960, Captain Joseph Kittinger accelerated through the thin air of the upper atmosphere to close to the speed of sound.

In four minutes and 38 seconds, Joseph Kittinger fell 25,820 m (84,711 ft) before his parachute opened – a drop equal to almost 68 Empire State Buildings, or three Mt Everests.

Empire State Building: 381 m (1,250 ft)

Mt Everest: 8,848 m (29,028 ft)

The wingspan of a Boeing 747 jumbo jet is 59.6 m (195.5 ft).

On its first flight, the Wright brothers' plane *Flyer* covered only 37 m (120 ft).

Hurrying into the history books

13:00

In 1978 Kenneth Warby broke the water speed record on Blowering Dam Lake in his hydroplane *Spirit of Australia*. The specially built powerboat went fast enough to cover the length of the world's longest river in about 13 hours.

At a top speed of 514 kph (319 mph), *Spirit of Australia* went fast enough to cover the 6,670 km (4,145 miles) of the Nile River in about 13 hours.

02:00

Fish left far behind

Measuring the speed of fish is not easy, mainly because no-one has yet organized a successful fish race. The gold medal would probably go to the sailfish, which can swim 100 m (328 ft) in little more than three seconds. In a race against *Spirit of Australia*, however, the sailfish would be left trailing.

| 0 | 100 kph (62 mph) | 200 kph (124 mph) | 300 kph (186 mph) | 400 kph (249 mph) | 500 kph (311 mph) |

Sailfish: 110 kph (68 mph)

Spirit of Australia: 514 kph (319 mph)

Marathon journeys by sea and air

Tales of long journeys have always had the power to fascinate. Legend has it that, some 2,500 years ago, an unknown messenger ran 36 km (22.5 miles) non-stop to Athens to bring news of a Greek victory on the battlefield at Marathon – a feat commemorated by the road race of the same name in the Olympic Games. Modern long-distance voyagers set themselves the ultimate challenge: to sail or fly around the world non-stop.

Hi there! By the time we land in Cape Town we will have flown nearly half a million times further than Orville Wright on his historic first flight!

In Germany, in 1972, Hans-Werner Grosse flew a glider non-stop for a record 1,461 km (908 miles).

In 1967 two Sikorsky HH-3E helicopters flew non-stop from New York to Paris, covering a record 6,874 km (4,271 miles). They took 30 hours and 46 minutes to complete the journey at an average speed of 223.5 kph (139 mph).

New York

Paris

In 1981 a helium-filled balloon called *Double Eagle V* flew non-stop from Nagashima, in Japan, to California, covering a record 8,383 km (5,209 miles).

A Boeing 747 jumbo jet flew non-stop from Paine Field, Washington, USA, to Cape Town, in South Africa, in 1976, covering a record distance for a passenger flight of 16,560 km (10,290 miles).

LAND AND WATER SPEED

HUMANS ARE FAST MOVERS on land and water – with a little help from a few mechanical friends. Unaided, we are real slowcoaches, and many animals can run and swim much faster. But we have always yearned to go faster and faster, and by using anything from horses to steam engines, from wind power to rockets, we have dramatically increased our speed on land and water. Such is our urge for speed that eventually all the current records will undoubtedly be broken by machines not even invented yet. The next tantalizing challenge on land is the magical barrier of 1,229 kph (764 mph) – the speed of sound.

Making tracks

On 3 July 1938 the British locomotive *Mallard* became the fastest steam train of all time. Pulling seven coaches, it reached 203 kph (126 mph) – more than four times the speed of Stevenson's *Rocket*.

Mallard steam train: 203 kph (126 mph)

LAND SPEEDS

Human speed on land was once restricted to running, riding, or using aids such as sledges and skis. But after the development of the railways, more than 150 years ago, speed quickly increased. For a century, trains set almost all the records. Only in the last 50 years have cars been able to beat them.

Cable-car: 35 kph (22 mph)

As fast as a bullet?

Not exactly... A rifle bullet travels at up to 2,635 kph (1,637 mph) – nearly 14 times the speed of Japan's *Bullet* train. However, it is one of the world's fastest railway services, with an average speed of 192 kph (119 mph), and a top speed of 230 kph (143 mph).

Champion cable-car

Travelling between Merida City and the top of Pico Espejo, in Venezuela, the *Teleférico Mérida* is the world's highest, longest, and fastest cable-car.

Rocket power

George Stevenson's *Rocket* was one of the earliest steam locomotives. With a top speed of 47 kph (29 mph), it was faster than any horse-drawn vehicle.

On the run

Top male athletes can sprint at up to 36 kph (22 mph), but are unable to run as fast over long distances.

Rocket steam train: 47 kph (29 mph)

Slowcoach

Horse-drawn stagecoaches were once a common form of transport in many parts of the world. Due to poor roads, their top speed was only 34 kph (21 mph).

Olympic runner: 36 kph (22 mph)

Stagecoach: 34 kph (21 mph)

WATER SPEEDS

Humans are slow swimmers – even an Olympic swimmer can reach only about 8 kph (5 mph). Thanks to the invention of powerboats and hydroplanes, however, we can now travel on water at nearly half the speed of sound.

Sailing out in front

Racing yachts can achieve average speeds of more than 18 kph (11 mph), although speeds of double this have been claimed for 19th-century sailing clippers. But the sail speed record was set in Canada in 1990 by the yacht *Longshot*, which reached nearly 69 kph (43 mph).

Longshot yacht: 69 kph (43 mph)

All pulling together

Crews in the UK's annual Oxford and Cambridge boat race row at an average speed of about 24 kph (15 mph) – three times the top speed of a human swimmer.

Dashing dolphins

Swimming in the wakes of ships, speedy dolphins can reach up to 59 kph (37 mph). Without this slipstream effect, their top speed is about 48 kph (30 mph).

Dolphin: 48 kph (30 mph)

Rowing eight: 24 kph (15 mph)

| 0 | 5 kph (3 mph) | 10 kph (6 mph) | 15 kph (9 mph) | 20 kph (12 mph) | 30 kph (19 mph) | 40 kph (25 mph) | 50 kph (31 mph) | 60 kph (37 mph) |

Bullet train:
average
speed
192 kph
(119 mph)

Intercity 225 train:
average speed
171 kph (106 mph)

Le Jamais Contente car:
106 kph (66 mph)

Never satisfied...

Le Jamais Contente (The Never
Satisfied), a torpedo-shaped
electric car driven by Camille
Jenatzy, broke the world land speed
record three times, at Achères, in
Paris, on 29 April 1899.

Hot on the rails

The *Intercity 225* is Britain's fastest scheduled
passenger train, averaging 171 kph (106 mph).

Formula One car:
235 kph (146 mph)

Pedal power

The top speed a cyclist has reached
without assistance is 89 kph (55 mph),
although slipstreaming behind another
vehicle to reduce wind resistance has
doubled this figure.

Racing cycle:
89 kph (55 mph)

Skateboard:
89 kph (55 mph)

Standing fast

The maximum speed reached by a
standing skateboarder is 89 kph (55 mph).
Even greater speeds have been recorded
when the rider lies down on the board
to reduce wind resistance.

Family car: top speed
161 kph (100 mph)

On the road

In the 1920s, when cars were
first mass-produced, a Model
T Ford had a top speed of
about 73 kph (45 mph).
Today, most standard
family cars are capable of
more than twice this speed.

Gone with the wind

The fastest sail-powered craft is not a yacht but a
sailboard. Thierry Bielak of France set the world
sail speed record on a sailboard in 1991.

The wind is so strong that I'm
travelling 10 times faster than
an Olympic swimmer.

Sailboard:
83 kph (52 mph)

Nuclear submarine:
83 kph (52 mph)

Catch me if you can, but
these boats are so fast I
can cover 4 km (2.5 miles)
in just one minute.

Submarine speed a secret

The top speed of Russian *Alfa*-class nuclear submarines remains
a closely guarded military secret, but it is believed that they are
capable of up to 83 kph (52 mph). Humans are still quite a bit
slower underwater than animals, however. The speedy sailfish
is 27 kph (17 mph) faster than this submarine.

Powerboat:
250 kph (155 mph)

70 kph (43 mph)   80 kph (50 mph)   90 kph (56 mph)   100 kph (62 mph)   200 kph (124 mp

SLOWCOACHES OF THE ANIMAL WORLD

Some animals are genuine slowcoaches, but others are handicapped by their tiny size. The top speed of about 5 kph (3 mph) of some cockroaches, for example, is actually a scorching 50 body lengths a second. If a racehorse could do this, it would be able to run at about 490 kph (304 mph) – three times the top speed of a family car.

Slow but sure
In the fable, the tortoise won the race against the hare. In real life, the tortoise is one of the slowest animals on land.

Slothful progress
Non-stop, it would take a sloth 24 years to stroll around the equator. As sloths sleep for up to 20 hours a day, however, the journey would actually take closer to 144 years.

A flurry of little legs
Large spiders in a hurry can scamper along at 1.8 kph (1.1 mph), but only for a few seconds.

Spider: 1.8 kph (1.1 mph)

Tortoise: 0.37 kph (0.23 mph)

Slow bird
The American woodcock is a real dawdler, flying just fast enough to stay in the air.

American woodcock: 8 kph (5 mph)

Harpy eagle: 60-80 kph (37-50 mph)

Swoop to kill
Birds of prey are at their fastest when diving. The fierce harpy eagle uses its speed to swoop down and pluck monkeys and sloths from the branches of trees.

Flight of fancy
Although higher speeds are often claimed by pigeon fanciers for their champion racing pigeons, it is unlikely that these birds can exceed 85 kph (53 mph). They are highly prized for their staying power over long distances, however.

Racing pigeon: 85 kph (53 mph)

Duck speed
Ducks are among the fastest birds in level flight, the mallard achieving a top recorded speed of 105 kph (65 mph).

Mallard duck: 105 kph (65 mph)

So fast, it's off the page...
The world's fastest bird – in level flight – is almost twice as fast as any shown here. You'll have to turn to page 42 to find out what it is...

Born to run
The fastest thoroughbred racehorses can gallop at nearly 70 kph (43 mph) over short distances – faster still without jockeys on their backs.

Who needs wings?
Although they are too heavy to fly, adult ostriches can outrun racehorses. Quite small chicks can reach 48 kph (30 mph). In South Africa, ostriches are even raced with jockeys on their backs.

On the hoof
Over short distances the pronghorn antelope of North America can run more than twice as fast as a charging African elephant.

On your marks, get set – gone!
The fastest of all land animals, the cheetah, can run at up to 100 kph (62 mph) over short distances. Its amazing acceleration is aided by claws that grip like the spikes of running shoes. If humans ran this fast, the world 100 m record would be a breathtaking 3.6 seconds.

Ostrich: 72 kph (45 mph)

Racehorse: 70 kph (43 mph)

Pronghorn antelope: 88 kph (55 mph)

Cheetah: 100 kph (62 mph)

Out of the blue
Speeds of more than 100 kph (62 mph) have been claimed by some people for the American bluefin tuna, but more reliable scientific tests suggest that 74 kph (46 mph) is its top speed.

Bluefin tuna: 74 kph (46 mph)

Marlin: 80 kph (50 mph)

Screaming reels
A favourite catch of deep-sea anglers, the speedy marlin can strip 100 m (328 ft) of line from a fishing reel in less than five seconds.

The fastest fish in the sea
The sailfish is the undisputed ocean sprint champion, with a recorded peak of 110 kph (68 mph) over short distances. At this speed it could dash the 50-m (164-ft) length of an Olympic swimming pool in only 1.6 seconds – 13 times faster than the quickest human.

Sailfish: 110 kph (68 mph)

70 kph (43 mph)   75 kph (47 mph)   80 kph (50 mph)   90 kph (56 mph)   100 kph (62 mph)   110 kph (68 mph)

AIR SPEED

HISTORY WAS MADE one winter morning in 1903, when two American bicycle mechanics towed a fragile timber and cloth aircraft on to a sandy North Carolina beach, started its noisy engine, and flew. The Wright brothers, Wilbur and Orville, were the world's first pilots, but their *Flyer* would have won no prizes for speed. It flew at only 48 kph (30 mph), and on its longest flight it took nearly one minute to cover only 260 m (852 ft). In 1967, only 64 years after the Wright brothers first flew, the X-15A-2 rocket plane flew more than 150 times faster. In the 59 seconds that the *Flyer* was airborne at Kill Devil Hills, Kitty Hawk, the X-15A-2 could have flown past Norfolk, Virginia, some 120 km (75 miles) away.

Speedy Spitfire
At the start of World War II (1939-45), the British Supermarine Spitfire was the world's fastest fighter aircraft. The fastest Spitfire, the Mk XIV, flew four times as fast as the natural world's fastest flyer, the spine-tailed swift.

Wright kite
The Wright brothers chose North Carolina's Outer Banks as the site to test their *Flyer* because the strong, steady winds there helped to lift the aircraft into the air, like a kite.

Flyer:
48 kph
(30 mph)

Westland *Lynx*:
400 kph (249 mph)

Three-winged fighter
Although no faster than the world's fastest bird, the Fokker Dr.I triplane was one of the most successful German fighter aircraft of World War I (1914-18). Flying a red-painted model, Manfred von Richthofen, the famous Red Baron, shot down 80 enemy planes.

Fokker Dr.I:
165 kph (103 mph)

Chop chop!
The world's fastest helicopter, the Westland *Lynx*, can fly at up to 400 kph (249 mph) – almost 14 times faster than the world's fastest insects, dragonflies. However, in normal use and fully loaded with 10 troops or two torpedoes, it cruises at about two-thirds of this speed.

Supermarine
Spitfire Mk XIV:
721 kph (448 mph)

Dawdling doodlebugs
V1 flying bombs, or doodlebugs, developed by Germany during World War II, were pilotless aircraft laden with explosives. Slower than fighter planes, they could be shot down, and less than half reached their targets.

V1 flying bomb:
563 kph
(350 mph)

Stately pioneer
Although slower than the top speed of a modern family car, the *Hindenburg* airship was the world's first transatlantic passenger service by air, crossing between Germany and the USA.

Hindenburg: cruising
speed 126 kph
(78 mph)

Silent swoopers
Gliders are unpowered aircraft that soar on rising currents of warm air. They can swoop at up to 320 kph (199 mph) – faster than the fastest motorcycle – but cruise at half this speed.

Glider:
320 kph
(199 mph)

Swift birds
Spine-tailed swifts can fly faster than any aircraft built before World War I.

Spine-tailed swift:
171 kph (106 mph)

Feathered flight
A skilled archer can fire a longbow arrow fast enough to spear the world's fastest helicopter.

Longbow arrow:
550 kph
(342 mph)

Keep pedalling!
Human-powered aircraft have huge wings to lift them into the air at very low speeds. In 1979, Bryan Allen pedalled *Gossamer Albatross* across the English Channel so slowly – half the speed of the Wright brothers' *Flyer* – that it barely cleared the waves.

Gossamer Albatross:
24 kph (15 mph)

Plunging birds
Peregrine falcons can dive as fast as the landing speed of a space shuttle.

Peregrine falcons can dive at 350 kph (217 mph).

Super sea-plane
From 1913-31, competition for the Schneider Trophy for sea-planes repeatedly raised the air speed record. After winning the final contest as the only entrant, the British Supermarine S.6B set a record of 610 kph (379 mph) – faster than a speeding arrow. Two weeks later it broke the 644 kph (400 mph) barrier. It was later modified into the Spitfire fighter.

Supermarine S.6B:
655 kph (407 mph)

Touchdown!
The speed of a space shuttle on landing is more than three times as fast as the top speed of the fastest land animal on Earth, the cheetah.

Space shuttle:
landing speed 350 kph (217 mph)

Cheetah: 100 kph (62 mph)

0	100 kph (62 mph)	200 kph (124 mph)	300 kph (186 mph)	400 kph (249 mph)	500 kph (311 mph)	600 kph (373 mph)

TGV train: top speed
515 kph (320 mph)

Railton Mobil Special car:
634 kph (394 mph)

The fastest train on the tracks

The French *Train à Grande Vitesse* (*TGV*), or High Speed Train, set the world record speed for a locomotive on 18 May 1990 when it reached 515 kph (320 mph) – more than 10 times the speed of *Rocket*. Its regular 246-kph (153-mph) journey between Massy and St Pierre is also the fastest scheduled rail service in the world.

Bluebird 2 car:
485 kph (301 mph)

Flat out

In 1935 Malcolm Campbell set another of his land speed records, this time in *Bluebird 2*. He reached 485 kph (301 mph) at Bonneville Salt Flats, Utah, USA.

Bird tops bike speed

In a steep dive to impress its mate, a male peregrine falcon can touch 350 kph (217 mph) – faster than the fastest motorcycle.

Peregrine falcon:
350 kph (217 mph)

Spirit of America – Sonic 1:
967 kph (600 mph)

Bluebird 1 car:
235 kph (146 mph)

Dragged to a halt

Drag cars travel so fast that they cannot be stopped by ordinary brakes, and have to use parachutes to slow them down. These cars race along a straight, 400-m (0.25-mile) course, accelerating from a standing start to three times the top speed of a family car.

First of nine

In 1924, Malcolm Campbell took his *Bluebird* car up to 235 kph (146 mph), the first of nine land speed records he was to set.

In the fast lane

The fastest Formula One circuit average of 235 kph (146 mph) was recorded by British driver Nigel Mansell in a Williams-Honda in the 1987 Austrian Grand Prix.

Motorcycle: almost
300 kph (186 mph)

Wheel-driven drag car:
497 kph (309 mph)

End of an era

Following in his father's footsteps, in 1964, at Lake Eyre, a salt waste in Australia, Donald Campbell reached 649 kph (403 mph) in his *Bluebird* car – setting the last ever wheel-driven world land speed record in the process.

Speedy superbikes

Modern motorcycles are more than three times as quick as the fastest bicycle. Japanese "superbikes" can reach top speeds of almost 300 kph (186 mph).

Bird on the water

In 1964, the same year he broke the world land speed record in his *Bluebird* car, Donald Campbell set a new world water speed record in his *Bluebird* speedboat, with a speed of 445 kph (277 mph).

Bluebird speedboat:
445 kph (277 mph)

Spirit of Australia hydroplane:
514 kph (319 mph)

Pacy powerboats

Powerboats certainly live up to their name, being capable of speeds of more than 250 kph (155 mph) – at least 10 times as fast as the eight-man rowing crews in the annual Oxford and Cambridge boat race.

Spirited skimmer

The official world water speed record is held by a hydroplane – a flat-bottomed motor boat that skims along the surface of the water. The record was set by Kenneth Warby on 8 October 1978, in *Spirit of Australia*.

SPEEDO 7

250 kph (155 mph)   275 kph (171 mph)   300 kph (186 mph)   400 kph (249 mph)   500 kph (311 mph)

Driverless sled dash

The unofficial land speed record, set by *Budweiser Rocket*, currently stands at 1,190 kph (739 mph), but this is not the fastest that a vehicle has ever travelled on land. In New Mexico in 1959, an unmanned US Air Force rocket sled on rails achieved the incredible speed of 4,972 kph (3,090 mph) – four times the speed of sound.

Budweiser Rocket reached 1,190 kph (739 mph) – less than a quarter the speed of the fastest unmanned vehicle on Earth.

At a speed of 4,972 kph (3,090 mph), this unmanned rocket sled could travel the 5,572 km (3,462 miles) between New York and London in just 67 minutes.

Special achievement

In 1947, British speed ace John Cobb, driving the streamlined *Railton Mobil Special*, set a new land speed record that stood for more than 15 years. He reached 634 kph (394 mph) – more than half the speed of sound.

Swift by name, swift by nature

Imagine that you are speeding along in a train. You look out of the window and see a bird flying alongside. Nothing unusual in that – but you might be surprised if you looked again a few minutes later and the bird was still there. It is not impossible – the aptly named spine-tailed swift can fly as fast as a British *Intercity 225*.

Both the spine-tailed swift and the *Intercity 225* can reach a speed of 171 kph (106 mph).

Into the jet age

In 1964, jet-powered cars took over from wheel-driven cars in the chase for the world land speed record. In 1965, Craig Breedlove of the USA became the first person to top 967 kph (600 mph), in his car *Spirit of America – Sonic 1*.

At this speed it would take me only four hours to travel the 3,936 km (2,446 miles) from Los Angeles to New York.

THE BLUE FLAME

Blue Flame car: 1,002 kph (622 mph)

Faster than a jumbo jet

American racer Gary Gabelich broke the world land speed record in his rocket-engined car, *Blue Flame*, on 23 October 1970 at Bonneville Salt Flats. His amazing speed of 1,002 kph (622 mph) was faster than a Boeing 747 jumbo jet.

Bluebird car: 649 kph (403 mph)

Approaching the speed of sound

The fastest man on wheels is American film stuntman Stan Barrett, who reached 1,190 kph (739 mph) in *Budweiser Rocket* on 17 December 1979 at Edwards Air Force Base, setting an unofficial world record. Extra thrust came from a sidewinder missile attached to the vehicle. Barrett's speed was only 39 kph (24 mph) short of the speed of sound.

Budweiser Rocket car: 1,190 kph (739 mph)

No contest

The sleepy sloth spends up to 20 hours a day dozing, and when it wakes moves at a truly slothful pace – a maximum speed of 0.19 kph (0.12 mph). The sloth's leisurely progress contrasts with that of the rapid French *TGV* train, which travels more than 1,294 times as fast as the sloth on its scheduled run, and 2,710 times as fast at record speed.

12:00 The sloth is in its starting blocks. A minute later it has moved 3 m (10 ft), while the *TGV* is 4 km (2.5 miles) down the track.

12:04 After four minutes, the sloth is half-way down the engine. The train, meanwhile, has travelled more than 16 km (10 miles).

12:07 The sloth takes more than seven minutes to crawl the 23-m (75-ft) length of the engine. In that time, the train has sped 29 km (18 miles) at its scheduled speed.

TGV

600 kph (373 mph)   700 kph (435 mph)   800 kph (497 mph)   900 kph (559 mph)   1,000 kph (621 mph)   1,100 kph (684 mph)   1,200 kph (746 mph)

On the far side of the Moon

In 1970, the crew of *Apollo 13* travelled the furthest anyone has ever travelled from Earth – 400,187 km (248,671 miles), which is more than 31 times the diameter of the planet. An explosion stopped *Apollo 13* from landing on the Moon. Instead, it had to return to Earth by swinging right around the Moon.

The diameter of the Earth is 12,756 km (7,926 miles).

At its furthest, Apollo 13 was more than 31 times as far away as the diameter of the Earth.

umbo jet-lag

At best, a five-hour stagecoach journey in the 18th century might cover a bumpy 60 km (37 miles). Now, allowing for refuelling, Concorde could fly you from London to Singapore in five hours. By jumbo, it actually takes more than twice as long, and while the flight might be smooth, you suffer jet-lag – tiredness caused by flying between very different time zones – for days afterwards.

In five hours, cruising at 2,179 kph (1,354 mph), Concorde could fly the 10,852 km (6,743 miles) between London and Singapore – about the same time it took an 18th-century stagecoach to cover 60 km (37 miles). If Concorde took off at 13:00 in London, therefore, it would be about 18:00 in London when it landed – in Singapore, however, it would be about 02:30 in the morning.

In five hours a Lamborghini *Diablo* – at 325 kph (202 mph) one of the world's fastest road cars – could cover the 1,531 km (951 miles) from Copenhagen, Denmark, to Rome.

Rome   Copenhagen

0   1,000 km (621 miles)

In five hours a French *TGV* high-speed train – top speed 515 kph (320 mph) – could cover the 2,486 km (1,545 miles) between Paris and Moscow.

Paris   Moscow

0   1,000 km (621 miles)   2,000 km (1,243 miles)

London

0   1,000 km (621 miles)   3,000 km (1,864 miles)   5,000 km (3,107 miles)   7,000 km (4,350 miles)   9,000 km (5,592 miles)

Singapore

Making tracks

In 1891 the Russian tsar began to build a railway line crossing his vast empire. Track was laid from both ends – west from Nakhodka, on the Sea of Japan, and east from Moscow. The world's longest continuous railway line, it goes nearly a quarter of the way around the globe.

Paris

0   2,000 km (1,243 miles)   4,000 km (2,486 miles)   6,000 km (3,728 miles)   8,000 km (4,971 miles)

Los Angeles

The Earth's equator measures 40,075 km (24,902 miles). Totalling 9,438 km (5,865 miles), the Trans-Siberian Railway stretches almost a quarter of the way around the world. It was finished in 1916, just one year before the Russian Revolution toppled the tsar.

The Trans-Siberian Railway is longer than the shortest distance between Paris and Los Angeles – 9,085 km (5,645 miles).

Supersonic flyers

"Supersonic" means faster than sound. Sound travels more slowly through the cool, thin air of the upper atmosphere. For aircraft, 1,062 kph (660 mph), or Mach 1, is used as the standard speed of sound at altitude. Mach 2 is twice the speed of sound, and so on.

Sound: Mach 1

Bell X-1 rocket plane: Mach 1

Apollo 10 at re-entry: Mach 37

Lockheed SR71A: Mach 3

X-15A-2: Mach 6

0   1,000 kph (621 mph)   3,000 kph (1,864 mph)   5,000 kph (3,107 mph)   7,000 kph (4,350 mph)   30,000 kph (18,642 mph)

Crossing America from coast to coast

American settlers heading west in their wagons in the 1840s and 1850s took about six hazardous months to cross the USA. Now the return journey can be done in air-conditioned comfort and safety in less than five hours by jumbo jet.

At 978 kph (608 mph) a jumbo jet can cover the distance between San Francisco and New York in four hours and 38 minutes.

At 6 kph (3.7 mph) it would take 31 days and nine hours to walk 4,517 km (2,807 miles), the distance between San Francisco and New York.

At 7,297 kph (4,534 mph) the X-15A-2 rocket plane could cover the distance between San Francisco and New York in less than 38 minutes.

San Francisco   50 kph (31 mph)   150 kph (93 mph)   900 kph (559 mph)   5,000 kph (3,107 mph)   New York

At 34 kph (21 mph) a stagecoach would take five days and 13 hours to travel 4,517 km (2,807 miles).

At 72 kph (45 mph) it would take a 1923 Model T Ford two days and 15 hours to travel 4,517 km (2,807 miles).

At 165 kph (103 mph) the *Empire State Express* could travel the distance from San Francisco to New York in less than 28 hours.

In 1986 a specially built plane, *Voyager*, became the first to fly non-stop around the world without refuelling. It landed back in California nine days, three minutes and 44 seconds after taking off.

GRAF ZEPPELIN

Graf Zeppelin was the first rigid airship to fly all the way around the world, in August 1929. It arrived back in New Jersey 21 days, five hours and 31 minutes after setting out, having flown at least 35,200 km (21,873 miles).

In 1968-69, in his boat *Suhaili*, Robin Knox-Johnson became the first person to sail, single-handedly, non-stop around the world. He covered a total of 48,478 km (30,122 miles) in 312 days.

20,000 km (12,428 miles)   25,000 km (15,535 miles)   30,000 km (18,642 miles)   35,000 km (21,749 miles)

For people in a hurry...

Concorde is the world's fastest passenger aircraft. Holding up to 130 passengers, it can fly from New York to London in under three hours. The same journey takes more than twice as long in an ordinary passenger aircraft.

Concorde: cruising speed 2,179 kph (1,354 mph)

Hi, down there! At this speed you could cross the Atlantic eight times in one day – although after the first few times you wouldn't know if you were coming or going!

X-15A-2 tops the lot

The fastest aircraft of all time, the 1960s North American X-15A-2, did not take off from a runway in the conventional way. Instead, a B-52 bomber ferried it to its cruising altitude, where its rocket engines blasted it to a maximum speed more than 150 times as fast as the Wright brothers' *Flyer*.

X-15A-2: maximum speed 7,297 kph (4,534 mph)

Yeager goes supersonic

Until the 1940s, many people believed that it would be impossible to fly faster than the speed of sound – about 1,229 kph (764 mph) near the ground, and 1,062 kph (660 mph) in the thinner upper atmosphere. Then, in 1947, American pilot Charles Yeager broke the sound barrier – Mach 1 – in a specially built, rocket-powered aircraft, the Bell X-1. Like the later X-15A and X-15A-2, the Bell X-1 was launched high in the air from a bomber.

Bell X-1: 1,128 kph (701 mph)

V2 rocket: 5,700 kph (3,542 mph)

Rocket bombs

Pioneering German rocket engineers built 3,610 V2 missiles towards the end of World War II. Aimed at cities, V2s travelled more than twice as fast as an ordinary rifle bullet.

Lockheed SR71A: 3,530 kph (2,193 mph)

U.S. AIR FORCE

Blackbird scorches speed record

The world air speed record for an aircraft taking off from the ground was set by the US Air Force in a Lockheed SR71A spy plane, in 1976. Nicknamed *Blackbird*, it flew more than 70 times as fast as the Wright brothers' *Flyer*.

Up, up and away!

Aviators aiming for record heights quickly run out of air. Balloonists need it to buoy up their gas-filled envelopes. Pilots control aircraft using the flow of air over rudder, ailerons, and elevators, but the record breaking X-15A also used tiny rockets for extra control in the thin air of the upper atmosphere.

BOEING 747

Boeing 747: cruising speed 978 kph (608 mph)

Cruising the skies

Boeing 747 jumbo jet passenger planes cruise at close to the speed of sound, and more than seven times as fast as the *Hindenburg* airship.

In August 1963, American test pilot Joseph Walker flew his X-15A over Edwards Air Force Base to 107,960 m (354,200 ft) – more than 12 times the height of Mt Everest.

In May 1961, Malcolm Ross and Victor Prather rose in a gas balloon from the deck of the USS *Antietam* to 34,668 m (113,740 ft) above the Gulf of Mexico – almost four times the height of Mt Everest.

Foxbat flies flat-out

Although designed back in the 1960s, the Russian MiG-25 is still the world's fastest combat aircraft. Nicknamed *Foxbat*, it can fly almost 10 times as fast as a diving peregrine falcon.

MiG-25: 3,395 kph (2,110 mph)

Fighter folds its wings

The main European combat aircraft, the Panavia *Tornado*, has wings that fold back during supersonic flight, much like the wings of a swooping spine-tailed swift. The *Tornado* is almost 14 times faster, however.

Tornado: 2,357 kph (1,465 mph)

Jet jumps into the air

By pointing the jet nozzles of the BAe *Harrier* downwards, the pilot can take off vertically, just like a bird. Swivelled to the horizontal position, the nozzles thrust the fighter plane forward to more than the speed of sound.

BAe *Harrier*: 1,190 kph (739 mph)

Shooting ahead

An ordinary rifle bullet flies fast enough to put a hole in all but the world's fastest fighter aircraft.

Back to the drawing board...

Power for the tiny Messerschmitt 163 *Komet* came from a single rocket, which accelerated it to almost twice the speed of an arrow. The plane had little impact on World War II, however, because it was uncontrollable at top speed, and ran out of fuel after only 10 minutes.

Me 163 *Komet*: 1,004 kph (624 mph)

Rifle bullet: 2,635 kph (1,637 mph)

Mt Everest: 8,848 m (29,028 ft)

700 kph (435 mph)	800 kph (497 mph)	900 kph (559 mph)	1,000 kph (621 mph)	2,000 kph (1,243 mph)	3,000 kph (1,864 mph)	4,000 kph (2,486 mph)	5,000 kph (3,107 mph)	6,000 kph (3,728 mph)	7,000 kph (4,350 mph)

GREAT CAPACITIES

IT IS EASIER TO GRASP the widths, heights, and lengths of things such as giant supertankers and sports stadiums than it is to imagine their volumes and capacities – the amount of space they contain, and how much of something it takes to fill that space. The reason is simple: when the width, height, and length of something doubles, its volume increases eightfold, not twofold. This rule explains the almost unbelievable fact that the fleet of lorries required to deliver enough standard containers to fill the huge Vehicle Assembly Building at the Kennedy Space Center would stretch as far as from Paris to Rome. It also explains the equally amazing fact that just one tower can hold enough water for someone to have a bath every day of the year for 65 years.

In case of another oil shortage...

Saudi Arabia is the world's largest oil producer, so it is not surprising that it also has the world's largest oil storage facilities. Each of the five colossal oil tanks at Ju'aymah is taller than a four-storey town house, and wider than the length of a soccer pitch. Each can hold 307,500,000 litres (67,641,882 gallons), or 1,500,000 barrels, of oil. If the oil were petroleum, each tank could hold enough for the average car to drive to the Moon and back about 6,000 times.

Each of the oil tanks at Ju'aymah is 22 m (72 ft) high and 118 m (387 ft) wide.

Four-storey town house: 20 m (66 ft) tall

One very big refinery

The largest oil refinery in the world is in Judibana, Falcón, Venezuela. The *Petroleos de Venezuela* can process 108,650,000 litres (23,900,131 gallons), or 530,000 barrels, of crude oil a day – one barrel being 205 litres (45 gallons). In one year, this is equivalent to refining all the oil in 61 large supertankers, each holding about 650,000,000 litres (142,982,840 gallons), or about 3,170,000 barrels – more than one supertanker a week.

In a year, *Petroleos de Venezuela* could process 193,450,000 barrels of crude oil.

Sixty-one large supertankers could carry 193,370,000 barrels of crude oil.

Supertankers swallow storage tanks

Even bigger than the largest container ships, the largest supertankers in the world can hold about 650,000,000 litres (142,982,840 gallons), or about 3,170,000 barrels, of oil – more than twice as much as one of the five giant storage tanks at Ju'aymah, in Saudi Arabia.

Two Ju'aymah tanks: 3,000,000 barrels of oil

Supertankers can be 485 m (1,591 ft) long and 70 m (230 ft) wide, and can carry 3,170,000 barrels of oil.

Four-storey town house: 20 m (66 ft) tall

Dresden Express, one of the world's largest container ships, is 294 m (965 ft) long and 40 m (131 ft) wide.

Space centre has lorryloads of room

Built in 1965 for the huge *Saturn V* rockets, the Vehicle Assembly Building at the Kennedy Space Center, Florida, USA, is one of the largest buildings in the world. It is 218 m (715 ft) long and 158 m (518 ft) wide, with one bay 160 m (525 ft) high, and another bay 64 m (210 ft) high. Its total volume is 3,664,993 cubic m (129,427,300 cubic ft) – room enough to stack about 100,000 standard containers. Were all the containers to be delivered on the same day, the queue of lorries would stretch about as far as from Paris to Rome.

One of the Vehicle Assembly Building's two bays is 160 m (525 ft) high.

Saturn V rocket: 111 m (364 ft) tall

20-m (66-ft) four-storey town house

Container lorry

Bath time – again

The waterspheroid water tower in Edmond, Oklahoma, in the USA, holds 1,893,000 litres (416,410 gallons) when full. Allowing 80 litres (17.5 gallons) for a bath, that is enough water for 23,663 baths – one every day of the year for 65 years.

Edmond waterspheroid: 49 m (161 ft) tall

Each tub represents about 500 baths

Hi! Only 23,662 more to go... I wonder if I've got enough soap?

The Edmond waterspheroid can hold enough water for 23,663 baths.

Four-storey town house: 20 m (66 ft)

Carrying containers by the thousand

Bulk products such as coal and wheat are carried loose in dry-cargo ships, but valuable goods such as clothes and electronic equipment are carried in container ships. Sealed metal containers allow all sorts of goods to be carried, without damage, by sea. Refrigerated containers allow even perishable goods, such as meat, to be carried all around the world. The more containers a ship can carry, the cheaper it is to move each container. Built in 1991, *Dresden Express*, one of the largest container ships in the world, has an overall capacity of 4,422 standard containers.

Dresden Express

Container lorry

A standard container is 6 m (20 ft) long, 2.4 m (8 ft) high, and 2.4 m (8 ft) wide, and is about 36 cubic m (1,280 cubic ft).

Paris

Allowing slightly more than 10 m (33 ft) for each lorry, 100,000 standard container lorries would stretch about as far as the 1,105 km (687 miles) from Paris to Rome.

Rome

Built in the 1930s, *Graf Zeppelin II* was 245 m (804 ft) long, and held almost 200,000 cubic m (7,062,895 cubic ft) of hydrogen. (Her sister airship, *Hindenburg*, was just as big.)

Gigantic gasholder

The world's largest gasholder, at Simmering, Vienna, Austria, is as tall as the largest living thing on Earth, the General Sherman giant sequoia. When full, it holds enough gas to fill either of the two largest airships ever built one-and-a-half times over. The same amount of gas could also fill four of the biggest-ever hot-air balloons, or 138 ordinary hot-air balloons.

Four-storey town house: 20 m (66 ft) tall

The General Sherman giant sequoia, in California, USA, is 84 m (276 ft) tall.

The Simmering gasholder is 84 m (276 ft) tall and holds 300,000 cubic m (10,594,342 cubic ft) of gas when full.

The largest hot-air balloon ever flown, the *Virgin Otsuka Pacific Flyer*, held 73,624 cubic m (2,600,000 cubic ft) of hot air. Richard Branson and Per Lindstrand flew it across the Pacific Ocean in 1991.

A standard hot-air balloon holds 2,180 cubic m (76,986 cubic ft) of hot air.

By the coachload

The capacities of single-decker buses and coaches vary around the world, but 49 passengers is about the average.

The average single-decker coach can hold 49 passengers.

Almost 12 coachloads of people are needed to fill a jumbo jet, at its maximum capacity.

By the jetload

The number of passenger seats that a Boeing 747 jumbo jet contains varies from airline to airline, and depends on the type of seats, how the seats are arranged, and the amount of room allowed for each passenger. The maximum number, however, is 570 – almost 12 coachloads.

The maximum passenger capacity of a jumbo jet is 570.

By the boatload

In addition to 350 cars and 60 lorries, the *Silja Europa* ferry, which operates between Finland and Sweden, can carry up to 3,000 passengers – more than five times as many as a jumbo jet.

The *Silja Europa* ferry is 30 m (98 ft) wide and 200 m (656 ft) long. It can hold 3,000 passengers.

It would take more than five jumbo jetloads of passengers to fill the *Silja Europa* ferry.

Pulling in the crowds

The *Circus Maximus* arena of ancient Rome is said to have held upwards of 250,000 people. The largest stadium in the modern world, the open Strahov Stadium, in Prague, in the Czech Republic, could hold about 240,000 spectators when it was completed in 1934 – more than twice as many as the world's biggest covered stadiums. It was built to accommodate mass gymnastics displays featuring up to 40,000 people performing in unison. To fill the Strahov Stadium would require 80 full *Silja Europa* ferries... or 421 full jumbo jets... or 4,898 full coaches.

When completed in 1934, the Strahov Stadium could hold 240,000 spectators.

It would take 80 full *Silja Europa* ferries to fill the Strahov Stadium.

BIG BUILDINGS

THE WORLD'S TALLEST building, or skyscraper, is the 110-storey, 443-m (1,453-ft) Sears Tower, in Chicago, in the USA. By the year 2001, however, it will have been overtaken by three new skyscrapers currently being built: the 452-m (1,483-ft) Petronas Tower, in Kuala Lumpur, Malaysia; the 457-m (1,500-ft) Chongqing Tower, in Chongqing, China; and, tallest of all, the 460-m (1,509-ft) Shanghai World Finance Centre, in Shanghai, China. But there are even higher structures, such as television masts. These are so tall and thin that they are not self-supporting – they are held up with strong cables called guy wires. The tallest structure ever built was a television mast near Warsaw, in Poland. It was a cloud-tickling 646 m (2,119 ft), but fell in 1991 while it was being repaired. As a result, the world's tallest structure is now the KTHI-TV mast in North Dakota, in the USA.

Head for heights
A four-storey town house is like a doll's house compared with the Statue of Liberty.

Viewing gallery in head

Statue of Liberty: 23 m (75 ft) from shoulders to torch

Four-storey town house: 20 m (66 ft)

Packing them in
Modern office buildings are designed to hold many people on large floor areas. If you draw St Peter's, the Empire State Building, and one of the two World Trade Center towers in proportion to how many people each can hold, you get this result.

World Trade Center tower: Completed 1973 Holds 25,000 people

Empire State Building: Completed 1931 Holds 15,000 people

St Peter's: Completed 1590 Holds 3,000 people

The corridors of power
St Peter's church would fit twice into the ground area occupied by the Great Pyramid. But both buildings are dwarfed by the vast floor area of the Pentagon, a US government building in Washington, DC. With its maze of corridors, the five-sided Pentagon is the largest office complex in the world.

Hello there – I'm lost! There are about 27 km (17 miles) of corridors here. That's a minimum four-hour walk. Help!

Pentagon: 117,355 sq m (1,263,240 sq ft)

Great Pyramid: 53,095 sq m (571,530 sq ft)

St Peter's: 36,446 sq m (392,310 sq ft)

Built to last
The Great Pyramid is almost entirely solid, so an immense amount of stone was used to build it – more than 2,500,000 cubic m (88,286,188 cubic ft). The same volume of brick and stone would build 40 Empire State Buildings.

40 Empire State Buildings

1 Great Pyramid

High office
At 243 m (797 ft), 1 Canada Square, at Canary Wharf, in London, is the UK's tallest office building. A chain of 8,000 paper clips dangled from the top floor would just about reach the ground.

1 Canada Square

Twin peaks
Cologne Cathedral, in Germany, has twin spires that are each 156 m (513 ft) high. When built, in the 1880s, they were the world's tallest artificial structures.

Desert wonder
It would take about 70 camels standing on each other's backs to reach the top of the Great Pyramid, at Giza, in Egypt. Built some 4,500 years ago as the tomb of King Khufu, it is 147 m (481 ft) high.

Missing top stone included in height

Great Pyramid

High church
With its enormous dome, St Peter's, in Rome, Italy, rises to 137.5 m (451 ft) – almost the length of two jumbo jets.

St Peter's

Lofty statue
The Statue of Liberty, in New York, in the USA, is 93 m (305 ft) high from the base of the pedestal to the torch.

Statue of Liberty

Toppling tower
At 55 m (180 ft), the Leaning Tower of Pisa, in Italy, is nearly three times as high as a four-storey town house.

Four-storey town house: 20 m (66 ft)

Leaning Tower

Cologne Cathedral

600 m (1,969 ft)

500 m (1,640 ft)

400 m (1,312 ft)

300 m (984 ft)

200 m (656 ft)

100 m (328 ft)

0

Put in their place
Compared with the world's great mountain ranges, such as the lofty Himalayas, even the tallest buildings are really very small indeed. It would take no fewer than 27 Eiffel Towers stacked one on top of the other to reach the peak of Mt Everest, the world's highest mountain. Even the tallest artificial structure in the world, North Dakota's KTHI-TV mast, would fit 14 times into the height of Everest. As for 20-m (66-ft), four-storey town houses, you would need no fewer than 443 of them to reach the top of the world's highest mountain.

27 Eiffel Towers

Mt Everest: 8,848 m (29,028 ft)

On a high wire
The KTHI-TV mast, in North Dakota, rises to 629 m (2,063 ft). Supported by guy wires, it is the tallest artificial structure in the world.

KTHI-TV mast

Standing tall
The world's highest self-supporting tower, at 553 m (1,815 ft), is the CN Tower, in Toronto, in Canada. It is five times as tall as the world's tallest tree.

THE ONLY WAY IS UP
Great advances in engineering mean modern buildings can be much taller than those of past centuries. Older buildings have solid, heavy walls, but today's skyscrapers have lightweight outer frameworks of steel and glass. The tallest modern buildings are in city centres. So many people want to live and work in city centres that skyscrapers are the only way to fit everyone in.

It's official
The world's tallest office building, the Sears Tower, in Chicago, is 443 m (1,453 ft) high – four times as tall as a *Saturn V* rocket.

CN Tower

High fliers
The World Trade Center, in New York, has two towers, the taller of which rises to 419 m (1,375 ft).

Sears Tower

Celebrity 'scraper
The world's best-known skyscraper is the 102-storey Empire State Building, in New York. It is 381 m (1,250 ft) tall, not counting the mast. Like other skyscrapers, it has warning beacons for low-flying aircraft.

World Trade Center

Empire State Building

Corporate structure
The Chrysler Building, in New York, is 319 m (1,046 ft) high to the top of its spire – equivalent to 60 of the city's famous yellow taxicabs stuck bumper to bumper in a traffic jam.

Chrysler Building

Towering success
At 321 m (1,052 ft) tall – including the radio mast – the Eiffel Tower, in Paris, France, is 16 times as tall as a 20-m (66-ft), four-storey town house. It was built for the 1889 Paris Exhibition, and remains a popular tourist attraction.

High finance
It would take a stack of 8,268 standard size (3.81-cm/1.5-in high) gold bars to reach the top of the 315-m (1,033-ft) tall Bank of China Building, in Hong Kong.

Bank of China Building

Eiffel Tower

I'm on the tower's second level. Only 952 more steps to the top – I think I'll take the lift!

600 m (1,969 ft)

500 m (1,640 ft)

400 m (1,312 ft)

300 m (984 ft)

200 m (656 ft)

100 m (328 ft)

0

Four-storey town house

Saturn V rocket: 111m (364 ft)

HUMAN POPULATION

A POPULATION EXPLOSION has seen the number of people in the world more than triple since 1900 – from less than 2,000,000,000 – to close to 6,000,000,000. Each day, enough people to fill the largest stadium in the modern world are added to the total. Thankfully, the world is a very big place. All the people in the world today could actually fit, standing shoulder to shoulder, on the small Indonesian island of Bali. Most of the world is only sparsely inhabited, and there are more people in some cities than there are in some of the largest countries. But nowhere do you find more people than in China – 20 per cent of all the people in the world live in this huge country.

Of the 5,734,000,000 or so people in the world, about 1,200,000,000 live in China. This means that, worldwide, one person in five lives in China.

There are more people in China today than there were in the whole world as recently as 150 years ago.

China grows and grows

China's population is bigger than that of any other country. Government policies now restrict couples in China from having more than one child, but even so it is predicted that the country's population will grow by another 60,000,000 by the year 2000.

China, the USA, and Australia mapped in proportion to their populations

Only about 18,000,000 people live in Australia, mainly in coastal cities. Large areas of this vast country are desert.

The population of the USA (including Alaska and Hawaii) is about 264,000,000 – 15 times bigger than that of Australia.

China's population of 1,200,000,000 is five times bigger than that of the USA, and 67 times bigger than that of Australia.

China's population in perspective

China covers an area only slightly greater than that of the USA, while Australia is not far behind China and the USA as one of the world's largest countries. However, the population of China is nearly five times greater than that of the USA, and an amazing 67 times greater than that of Australia. When the maps of these three countries are redrawn to a scale in proportion to their populations, rather than their actual areas, you can see just how vast the population of China really is.

Australia is the fifth largest country in the world – after Russia, Canada, China, and the USA – but has a population no bigger than that of Sri Lanka.

Land and people...

Japan and Zimbabwe are countries with almost exactly the same land areas, but with very different populations. In terms of population, it would take 11.5 Zimbabwes to equal one Japan.

The population of Japan is about 125,000,000.

The population of Zimbabwe is about 11,000,000.

People and land...

Australia and Sri Lanka are countries with similar populations, but Sri Lanka would fit into Australia 119 times. If Australia were as densely populated as Sri Lanka, Australia's population would be more than 2,000,000,000. If Sri Lanka were as sparsely populated as Australia, Sri Lanka's population would be only about 150,000.

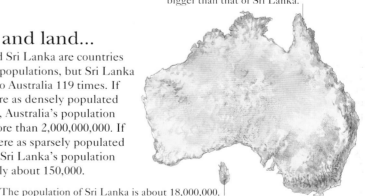

The population of Sri Lanka is about 18,000,000.

Size by area

In this box, all the countries featured on these two pages are drawn in proportion to their actual size, in area.

China: 9,596,960 sq km (3,705,676 sq miles)

USA: 9,529,063 sq km (3,679,459 sq miles)

Australia: 7,836,848 sq km (3,026,044 sq miles)

Sudan: 2,505,813 sq km (967,570 sq miles)

Zimbabwe: 390,580 sq km (150,815 sq miles)

Japan: 377,800 sq km (145,880 sq miles)

South Korea: 99,020 sq km (38,235 sq miles)

Sri Lanka: 65,610 sq km (25,334 sq miles)

Bali: 5,620 sq km (2,170 sq miles)

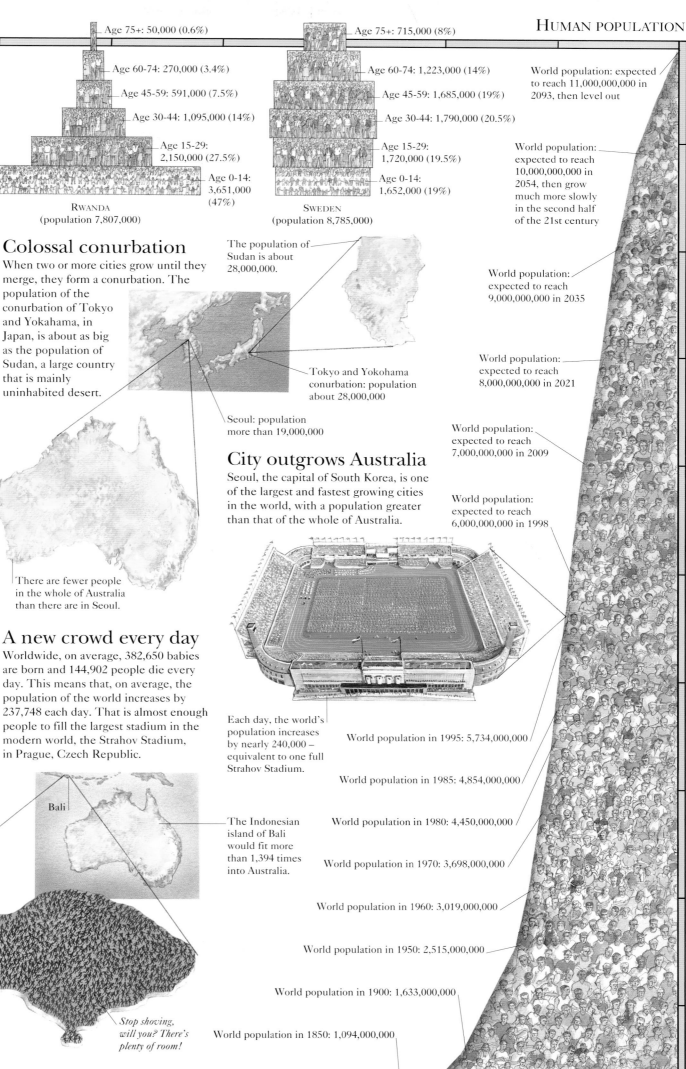

Population pyramids

Living standards in a country are reflected in the age structure of its population. In poor countries, families tend to be large, but few people survive to old age. In rich countries, by contrast, families tend to be small, and better living conditions mean that many more people survive to old age. The difference is clear if you look at the age structures of Rwanda, a poor country, and Sweden, a rich one, as "population pyramids". These two countries have similar total populations, but very different numbers of young and old people.

Age 75+: 50,000 (0.6%)

Age 60-74: 270,000 (3.4%)

Age 45-59: 591,000 (7.5%)

Age 30-44: 1,095,000 (14%)

Age 15-29: 2,150,000 (27.5%)

Age 0-14: 3,651,000 (47%)

RWANDA
(population 7,807,000)

Age 75+: 715,000 (8%)

Age 60-74: 1,223,000 (14%)

Age 45-59: 1,685,000 (19%)

Age 30-44: 1,790,000 (20.5%)

Age 15-29: 1,720,000 (19.5%)

Age 0-14: 1,652,000 (19%)

SWEDEN
(population 8,785,000)

Crowding the court

All cities are crowded, but some are more crowded than others. Take the population densities of London and Hong Kong Island. Hong Kong Island is so closely packed that if it were divided into tennis courts there would be 25 people on each court. In London there would be only one person on each court.

Hong Kong Island: 25 people in an area the size of a tennis court

A tennis court covers 261 sq m (2,808 sq ft).

London: one person in an area the size of a tennis court

The world on an island

Allowing about 1 sq m (10.8 sq ft) per person, all the people in the world could stand shoulder to shoulder on the Indonesian island of Bali. The biggest problem would be getting them all there...

Bali has an area of about 5,620,000,000 sq m (60,495,156,000 sq ft) – slightly less than 1 sq m (10.8 sq ft) for each of the 5,734,000,000 people on Earth.

Stop shoving, will you? There's plenty of room!

Colossal conurbation

When two or more cities grow until they merge, they form a conurbation. The population of the conurbation of Tokyo and Yokahama, in Japan, is about as big as the population of Sudan, a large country that is mainly uninhabited desert.

The population of Sudan is about 28,000,000.

Tokyo and Yokahama conurbation: population about 28,000,000

Seoul: population more than 19,000,000

City outgrows Australia

Seoul, the capital of South Korea, is one of the largest and fastest growing cities in the world, with a population greater than that of the whole of Australia.

There are fewer people in the whole of Australia than there are in Seoul.

A new crowd every day

Worldwide, on average, 382,650 babies are born and 144,902 people die every day. This means that, on average, the population of the world increases by 237,748 each day. That is almost enough people to fill the largest stadium in the modern world, the Strahov Stadium, in Prague, Czech Republic.

Each day, the world's population increases by nearly 240,000 – equivalent to one full Strahov Stadium.

Bali

The Indonesian island of Bali would fit more than 1,394 times into Australia.

Accelerated growth

The population of the world in 1500 was about 460,000,000, after centuries of slow growth. It then grew steadily until the middle of the 19th century, when it passed 1,000,000,000. It then began the incredible rise that has already enlarged it to more than 12 times the 1500 figure. In another 100 years it could almost double, to close to 11,000,000,000.

World population in 1500: 460,000,000

World population in 1600: 579,000,000

World population in 1700: 679,000,000

World population in 1800: 954,000,000

World population in 1850: 1,094,000,000

World population in 1900: 1,633,000,000

World population in 1950: 2,515,000,000

World population in 1960: 3,019,000,000

World population in 1970: 3,698,000,000

World population in 1980: 4,450,000,000

World population in 1985: 4,854,000,000

World population in 1995: 5,734,000,000

World population: expected to reach 6,000,000,000 in 1998

World population: expected to reach 7,000,000,000 in 2009

World population: expected to reach 8,000,000,000 in 2021

World population: expected to reach 9,000,000,000 in 2035

World population: expected to reach 10,000,000,000 in 2054, then grow much more slowly in the second half of the 21st century

World population: expected to reach 11,000,000,000 in 2093, then level out

WORLD POPULATION (IN BILLIONS)

1500   1600   1700   1800   1900   2000   2100

YEAR

GROWTH AND AGE

"GREAT OAKS FROM little acorns grow." It is one of the marvels of nature that nearly all living things increase in size, often by a phenomenal factor of many millions from the seed or egg from which they originated. This growth can be extremely rapid and quite short-lived, or it can be very slow and extended over many years – over many centuries, even. Bamboo can grow as much in one day as one species of evergreen shrub might grow in 1,000 or more years. No animal lives anywhere near as long as the longest-lived trees or plants. Given the right conditions, however, some creatures can live for a surprisingly long time – including us humans, for whom a life span of 100 years is nowadays by no means unusual.

Bamboo shoots up twice as fast

Pacific giant kelp, a kind of seaweed, can grow as much as 45 cm (18 in) in one day. If you think that is a lot, try bamboo. Bamboo can grow at twice that rate – by the height of the average two-year-old child in one day. Bamboo grows so fast because it is actually a kind of grass found in tropical and semi-tropical countries with very high rainfalls – just think how the grass always seems to need cutting after a heavy downpour. Bamboo might grow twice as fast as Pacific giant kelp, but the kelp can eventually grow to twice the size of bamboo – and 34 times the height of the average man.

Pacific giant kelp can grow 45 cm (18 in) in one day.

Bamboo can grow 90 cm (3 ft) in one day.

The average two-year-old child is 84 cm (2 ft 9 in) tall.

Pacific giant kelp can grow to 60 m (197 ft) – 34 times the height of the average man.

Bamboo can grow to 30 m (98 ft).

High and mighty

The tallest tree in the world is a coast redwood in Humboldt Redwoods State Park, California. Standing 110.6 m (363 ft) high, it is 17.6 m (58 ft) taller than the Statue of Liberty, and nearly twice as big as fully grown Pacific giant kelp. However, much taller eucalyptus trees were recorded in Australia in the 19th century – trees that were more than 130 m (426 ft) high.

Coast redwood: 110.6 m (363 ft) from base of trunk to top of tree

Statue of Liberty: 93 m (305 ft) from base of pedestal to torch

Shrub grows ever so slowly

A 120-year-old specimen of *Dioon edule*, an evergreen shrub found in Mexico, was just 10 cm (4 in) tall, and growing at an almost imperceptible 0.76 mm (0.03 in) a year. At that rate it would take 1,184 years to grow as much as bamboo can grow in one day.

100 years

50 years

I think I'm going to need a bigger lawn mower!

The average man is 1.75 m (5 ft 9 in) tall.

One specimen of *Dioon edule* was found to be growing at only 0.76 mm (0.03 in) a year.

Pacific giant kelp: up to 60 m (197 ft)

Ancient trees outlive humans and animals

Most animals live much longer in captivity than they do in the wild, because in captivity they are well fed, receive regular medical attention, and are safe from predators. Over the years, human life expectancy has increased steadily, mainly because of advances in medicine. Today it is highest in rich, industrialized countries with good diets, and lowest in poor countries. We still have a long way to go to catch up the longest lived trees, however, which can live for 50 times as long as the oldest humans.

Women generally live longer than men. The average life expectancy for women in the USA is 75 years, and there are increasing numbers living for more than 100 years.

The average life expectancy for men in the USA is 72 years.

Chimpanzee: up to 53 years

Hippopotamus: up to 54 years

Eagle owl: up to 68 years

Indian elephant: up to 77 years

Dolphin: up to 65 years

Rhinoceros: up to 50 years

Mouse: up to six years

Trout: up to 10 years

Rabbit: up to 13 years

Dog: up to 20 years

Tiger: up to 26 years

Cow: up to 30 years

Polar bear: up to 38 years

Bison: up to 40 years

| 0 | 10 years | 20 years | 30 years | 40 years | 50 years | 60 years | 70 years | 80 years |

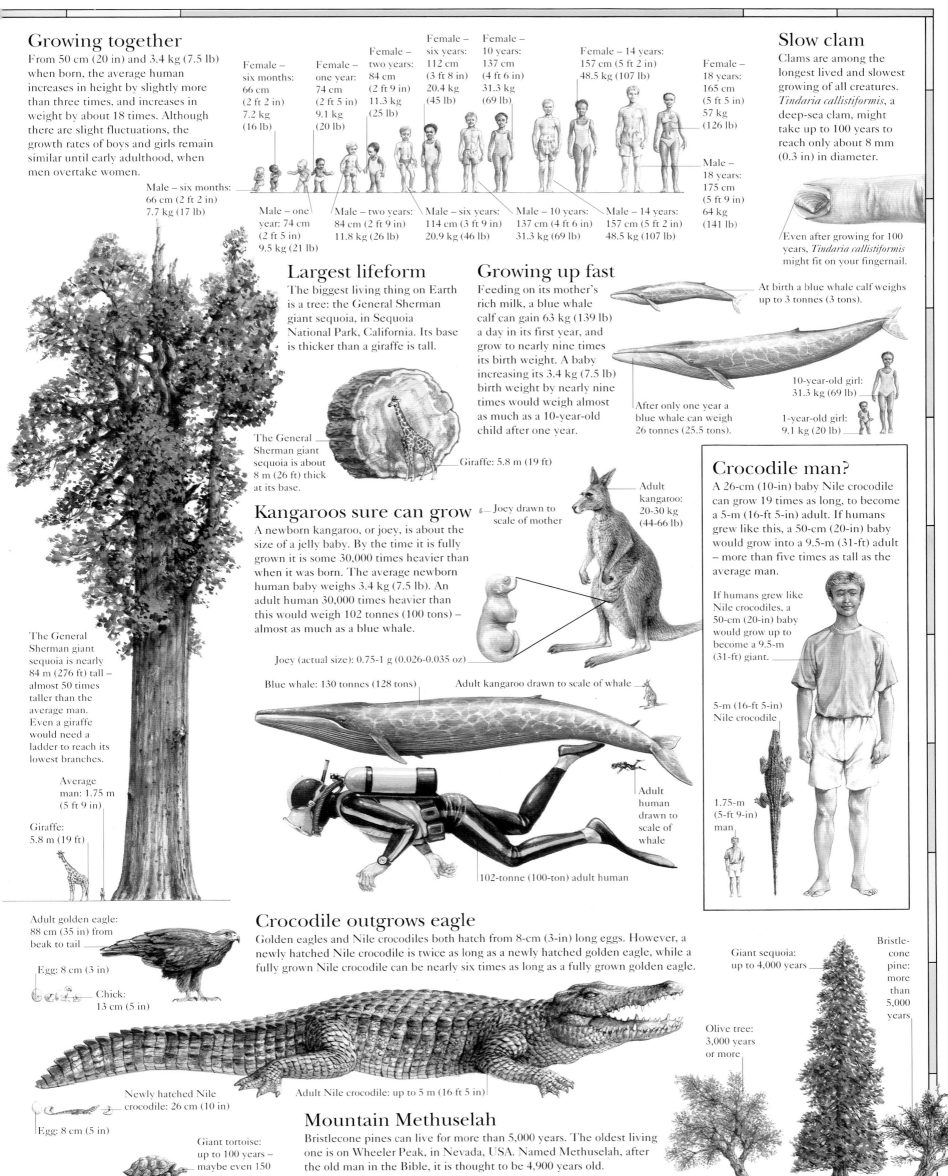

Growing together

From 50 cm (20 in) and 3.4 kg (7.5 lb) when born, the average human increases in height by slightly more than three times, and increases in weight by about 18 times. Although there are slight fluctuations, the growth rates of boys and girls remain similar until early adulthood, when men overtake women.

Female – six months: 66 cm (2 ft 2 in) 7.2 kg (16 lb)

Female – one year: 74 cm (2 ft 5 in) 9.1 kg (20 lb)

Female – two years: 84 cm (2 ft 9 in) 11.3 kg (25 lb)

Female – six years: 112 cm (3 ft 8 in) 20.4 kg (45 lb)

Female – 10 years: 137 cm (4 ft 6 in) 31.3 kg (69 lb)

Female – 14 years: 157 cm (5 ft 2 in) 48.5 kg (107 lb)

Female – 18 years: 165 cm (5 ft 5 in) 57 kg (126 lb)

Male – 18 years: 175 cm (5 ft 9 in) 64 kg (141 lb)

Male – six months: 66 cm (2 ft 2 in) 7.7 kg (17 lb)

Male – one year: 74 cm (2 ft 5 in) 9.5 kg (21 lb)

Male – two years: 84 cm (2 ft 9 in) 11.8 kg (26 lb)

Male – six years: 114 cm (3 ft 9 in) 20.9 kg (46 lb)

Male – 10 years: 137 cm (4 ft 6 in) 31.3 kg (69 lb)

Male – 14 years: 157 cm (5 ft 2 in) 48.5 kg (107 lb)

Slow clam

Clams are among the longest lived and slowest growing of all creatures. *Tindaria callistiformis*, a deep-sea clam, might take up to 100 years to reach only about 8 mm (0.3 in) in diameter.

Even after growing for 100 years, *Tindaria callistiformis* might fit on your fingernail.

Largest lifeform

The biggest living thing on Earth is a tree: the General Sherman giant sequoia, in Sequoia National Park, California. Its base is thicker than a giraffe is tall.

The General Sherman giant sequoia is about 8 m (26 ft) thick at its base.

Giraffe: 5.8 m (19 ft)

Growing up fast

Feeding on its mother's rich milk, a blue whale calf can gain 63 kg (139 lb) a day in its first year, and grow to nearly nine times its birth weight. A baby increasing its 3.4 kg (7.5 lb) birth weight by nearly nine times would weigh almost as much as a 10-year-old child after one year.

At birth a blue whale calf weighs up to 3 tonnes (3 tons).

After only one year a blue whale can weigh 26 tonnes (25.5 tons).

10-year-old girl: 31.3 kg (69 lb)

1-year-old girl: 9.1 kg (20 lb)

Kangaroos sure can grow

A newborn kangaroo, or joey, is about the size of a jelly baby. By the time it is fully grown it is some 30,000 times heavier than when it was born. The average newborn human baby weighs 3.4 kg (7.5 lb). An adult human 30,000 times heavier than this would weigh 102 tonnes (100 tons) – almost as much as a blue whale.

Joey drawn to scale of mother

Adult kangaroo: 20-30 kg (44-66 lb)

Joey (actual size): 0.75-1 g (0.026-0.035 oz)

Blue whale: 130 tonnes (128 tons)

Adult kangaroo drawn to scale of whale

Adult human drawn to scale of whale

102-tonne (100-ton) adult human

Crocodile man?

A 26-cm (10-in) baby Nile crocodile can grow 19 times as long, to become a 5-m (16-ft 5-in) adult. If humans grew like this, a 50-cm (20-in) baby would grow into a 9.5-m (31-ft) adult – more than five times as tall as the average man.

If humans grew like Nile crocodiles, a 50-cm (20-in) baby would grow up to become a 9.5-m (31-ft) giant.

5-m (16-ft 5-in) Nile crocodile

1.75-m (5-ft 9-in) man

The General Sherman giant sequoia is nearly 84 m (276 ft) tall – almost 50 times taller than the average man. Even a giraffe would need a ladder to reach its lowest branches.

Average man: 1.75 m (5 ft 9 in)

Giraffe: 5.8 m (19 ft)

Crocodile outgrows eagle

Golden eagles and Nile crocodiles both hatch from 8-cm (3-in) long eggs. However, a newly hatched Nile crocodile is twice as long as a newly hatched golden eagle, while a fully grown Nile crocodile can be nearly six times as long as a fully grown golden eagle.

Adult golden eagle: 88 cm (35 in) from beak to tail

Egg: 8 cm (3 in)

Chick: 13 cm (5 in)

Newly hatched Nile crocodile: 26 cm (10 in)

Egg: 8 cm (5 in)

Adult Nile crocodile: up to 5 m (16 ft 5 in)

Giant sequoia: up to 4,000 years

Bristlecone pine: more than 5,000 years

Olive tree: 3,000 years or more

Mountain Methuselah

Bristlecone pines can live for more than 5,000 years. The oldest living one is on Wheeler Peak, in Nevada, USA. Named Methuselah, after the old man in the Bible, it is thought to be 4,900 years old.

Giant tortoise: up to 100 years – maybe even 150

90 years   100 years   3,000 years   4,000 years   5,000 years

THE HUMAN BODY

THE AMAZING MACHINE that is the human body is full of surprises. Spread out flat, the average adult's skin is large enough to cover 10 copies of this book, front and back, while the air sacs in the lungs of three adults could cover a whole tennis court. Bone can withstand tremendous forces, but it is surprisingly light – when walking, the average adult presses down on each thighbone with the weight of an elephant, yet the whole skeleton accounts for only a sixth of the body's total weight. But perhaps the most remarkable organ in the human body is the brain, which triples in weight between birth and adulthood, until it weighs as much as the heart and both lungs put together. In relation to body size, the human brain is larger than the brain of any animal on Earth.

Your body – the inside story

Most of us have only a vague idea of the locations of the main organs inside our bodies. For example, most people think the heart is on the left side of the chest, when in fact it is located centrally, between the lungs.

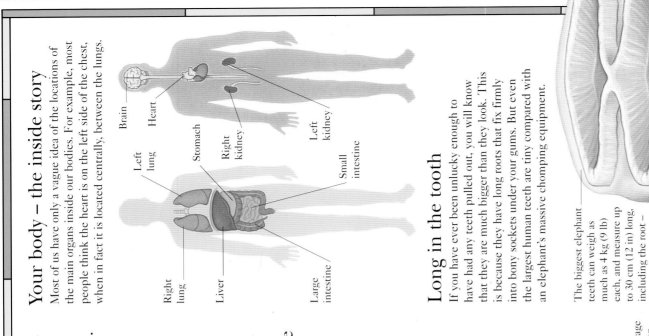

Brain

Heart

Left lung

Stomach

Right kidney

Left kidney

Right lung

Liver

Small intestine

Large intestine

Long in the tooth

If you have ever been unlucky enough to have had any teeth pulled out, you will know that they are much bigger than they look. This is because they have long roots that fix firmly into bony sockets under your gums. But even the largest human teeth are tiny compared with an elephant's massive chomping equipment.

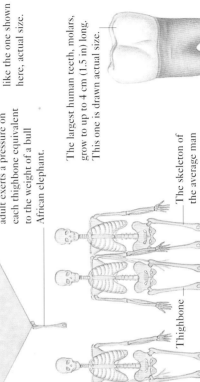

The biggest elephant teeth can weigh as much as 4 kg (9 lb) each, and measure up to 30 cm (12 in) long, including the root – like the one shown here, actual size.

The largest human teeth, molars, grow to up to 4 cm (1.5 in) long. This one is drawn actual size.

Big bones, little bones

You are born with about 300 bones in your body. As you grow, some of them fuse, until you have about 200 as an adult. The biggest bones, the thighbones, or femurs, are more than 150 times as long as the smallest, the stirrup bone, or stapes, inside each ear.

The average adult's thighbones are about 50 cm (20 in) long. This one is drawn actual size.

Grain of rice (actual size)

The average adult's stirrup bones are 3 mm (0.1 in) long – about as big as a grain of rice.

Bone can bear the weight

Bone is immensely strong – but then it needs to be. When walking, with each step an adult of average weight exerts a downward pressure on each thighbone of about 844 kg per sq cm (12,000 lb per sq in). Given that the thinnest part of the thighbone is about 2.5 cm (1 in) thick, this is equivalent to the weight of a bull African elephant. When running and jumping, the pressure on the thighbones is even greater.

A bull African elephant weighs about 5 tonnes (5 tons).

When walking, the average adult exerts a pressure on each thighbone equivalent to the weight of a bull African elephant.

Light as bone

Although bone is extremely strong, it is surprisingly light, accounting for only about a sixth of the average adult's overall body weight. Put another way, one person weighs the same as six skeletons – even more if that person is overweight.

The skeleton of the average man weighs only about 11 kg (24 lb).

Thighbone

The average man weighs 64 kg (141 lb) – as much as six skeletons.

50 cm (20 in)

35 cm (14 in)

30 cm (12 in)

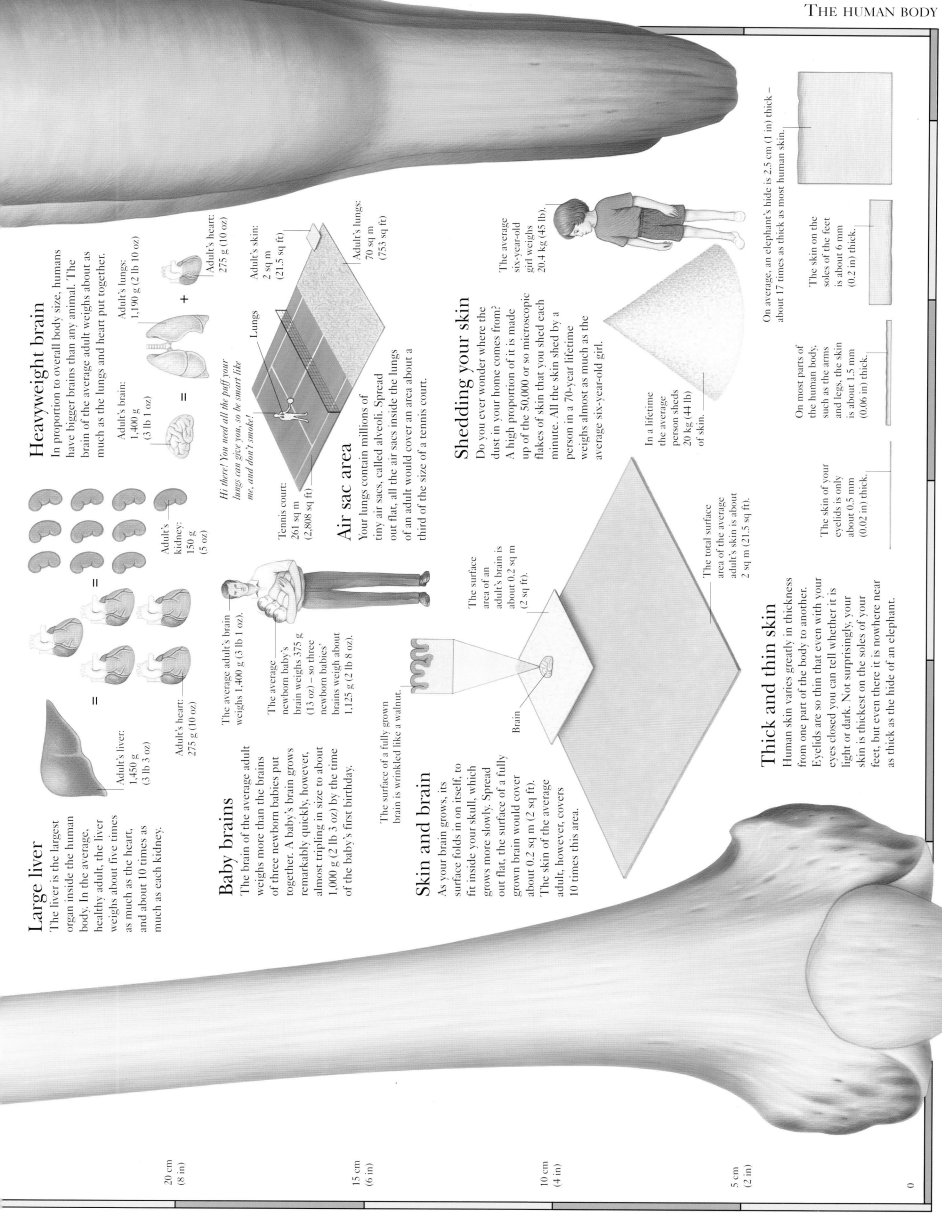

Large liver

The liver is the largest organ inside the human body. In the average, healthy adult, the liver weighs about five times as much as the heart, and about 10 times as much as each kidney.

Adult's liver:
1,450 g
(3 lb 3 oz)

Adult's heart:
275 g (10 oz)

Adult's kidney:
150 g
(5 oz)

Heavyweight brain

In proportion to overall body size, humans have bigger brains than any animal. The brain of the average adult weighs about as much as the lungs and heart put together.

Adult's brain:
1,400 g
(3 lb 1 oz)

Adult's lungs:
1,190 g (2 lb 10 oz)

Adult's heart:
275 g (10 oz)

Baby brains

The brain of the average adult weighs more than the brains of three newborn babies put together. A baby's brain grows remarkably quickly, however, almost tripling in size to about 1,000 g (2 lb 3 oz) by the time of the baby's first birthday.

The average adult's brain weighs 1,400 g (3 lb 1 oz).

The average newborn baby's brain weighs 375 g (13 oz) – so three newborn babies' brains weigh about 1,125 g (2 lb 8 oz).

Skin and brain

As your brain grows, its surface folds in on itself, to fit inside your skull, which grows more slowly. Spread out flat, the surface of a fully grown brain would cover about 0.2 sq m (2 sq ft). The skin of the average adult, however, covers 10 times this area.

The surface of a fully grown brain is wrinkled like a walnut.

The surface area of an adult's brain is about 0.2 sq m (2 sq ft).

Brain

Air sac area

Your lungs contain millions of tiny air sacs, called alveoli. Spread out flat, all the air sacs inside the lungs of an adult would cover an area about a third of the size of a tennis court.

Hi there! You need all the puff your lungs can give you, so be smart like me, and don't smoke!

Lungs

Tennis court:
261 sq m
(2,808 sq ft)

Adult's lungs:
70 sq m
(753 sq ft)

Adult's skin:
2 sq m
(21.5 sq ft)

Shedding your skin

Do you ever wonder where the dust in your home comes from? A high proportion of it is made up of the 50,000 or so microscopic flakes of skin that you shed each minute. All the skin shed by a person in a 70-year lifetime weighs almost as much as the average six-year-old girl.

The average six-year-old girl weighs 20.4 kg (45 lb).

In a lifetime the average person sheds 20 kg (44 lb) of skin.

The total surface area of the average adult's skin is about 2 sq m (21.5 sq ft).

Thick and thin skin

Human skin varies greatly in thickness from one part of the body to another. Eyelids are so thin that even with your eyes closed you can tell whether it is light or dark. Not surprisingly, your skin is thickest on the soles of your feet, but even there it is nowhere near as thick as the hide of an elephant.

The skin of your eyelids is only about 0.5 mm (0.02 in) thick.

On most parts of the human body, such as the arms and legs, the skin is about 1.5 mm (0.06 in) thick.

On average, an elephant's hide is 2.5 cm (1 in) thick – about 17 times as thick as most human skin.

The skin on the soles of the feet is about 6 mm (0.2 in) thick.

20 cm
(8 in)

15 cm
(6 in)

10 cm
(4 in)

5 cm
(2 in)

0

THE BODY AT WORK

ADVANCES IN MEDICAL SCIENCE mean that many of us can now expect to enjoy long, relatively healthy lives of 70 years or more. But nothing in medical science can match the natural miracle that sees us grow from a dot-size fertilized egg into a fully developed baby in the space of just 40 weeks. We are born with all our organs in full working order, and for most of us they will last, largely unaided, until our dying day. By then, they will have performed some incredible feats. Our lungs will have inhaled and exhaled enough air to fill either of the two largest airships ever built almost one-and-a-half times over. Our hearts will have beaten more than 2,500,000,000 times – pumping enough blood around the body to fill the fuel tanks of 700 jumbo jets in the process – and our stomachs and intestines will have digested the weight of six bull African elephants or more in food.

Every breath you take

When you do something strenuous, such as swimming or running, you breathe deeply and rapidly. At rest, you take shallower, less frequent breaths. When breathing normally, however, you take in about 500 cubic cm (30.5 cubic in) of air with each breath, at an average rate of 15 breaths a minute. Based on normal breathing, in a 70-year lifetime you will breathe about 275,000 cubic m (9,711,481 cubic ft) of air – enough to fill either of the two largest airships ever built almost one-and-a-half times over.

Every beat of your heart

Your heart is an amazingly strong and hard-wearing muscle. On average, it beats 70 times a minute, and pumps 59 cubic cm (3.6 cubic in) of blood with each beat. In a 70-year lifetime, that works out at more than 2,500,000,000 beats, pumping about 152,000,000 litres (33,435,987 gallons) of blood – enough to fill the fuel tanks of 10 Boeing 747 jumbo jets every year.

Elephantine appetites

The amount of food that people eat varies from person to person and from country to country, but in a 70-year lifetime the average person in a rich country such as the USA eats an estimated 30 tonnes (29.5 tons) of food – the weight of six bull African elephants.

A bull African elephant weighs about 5 tonnes (5 tons) – so six of them weigh about 30 tonnes (29.5 tons).

The average man weighs 64 kg (141 lb). If he eats 30 tonnes (29.5 tons) of food in a 70-year lifetime, that works out at 469 times his adult body weight.

Like her sister ship *Hindenburg*, the 1930s airship *Graf Zeppelin II* was 245 m (804 ft) long, and held about 200,000 cubic m (7,062,895 cubic ft) of hydrogen. In a 70-year lifetime, the average person breathes enough air to fill *Graf Zeppelin II* almost one-and-a-half times over.

Hi! I think I'll stick to blowing up party balloons in future!

When full, the fuel tanks of a jumbo jet hold 217,000 litres (47,734 gallons).

Your heart beats faster when you exercise, and slower when you rest, but on average it beats 70 times a minute.

Vast area of vessels

As well as larger veins and arteries, your body contains millions of tiny blood vessels called capillaries. Minute tubes, each slightly more than 1 mm (0.04 in) long, they carry blood to all parts of your body. All the capillaries in the average adult's body form a huge network that, if spread out flat, would cover about 5,000 sq m (53,821 sq ft) – an area greater than that covered by 19 tennis courts.

All the capillaries in the average adult's body could cover an area greater than 19 tennis courts.

Fist-size filters

You have two kidneys, each about the size of a clenched fist. They filter waste products and excess water from your blood, then pass these on to your bladder in the form of urine. Although the kidneys of the average adult filter about 1.2 litres (2.1 pints) of blood every minute of the day, they only extract about 1.4 litres (2.5 pints) of urine each day.

The kidneys of the average adult weigh about 150 g (5 oz) each, and are about the size of a clenched fist.

Every minute, the kidneys of the average adult filter about 1.2 litres (2.1 pints) of blood.

Each day, the kidneys of the average adult extract about 1.4 litres (2.5 pints) of urine from the blood.

2 litres (3.5 pints)

1 litre (1.8 pints)

0

The blood in your body

Blood might be thicker than water, but even a few drops of it can spread over a surprisingly large area – as you will know if you have ever cut yourself badly. Being generally smaller, women usually have less blood than men. When pregnant, however, a woman produces extra blood to supply her growing baby.

A pregnant woman has up to 6.5 litres (11.4 pints) of blood.

A fully grown woman has about 4.5 litres (7.9 pints) of blood.

A fully grown man has about 5 litres (8.8 pints) of blood.

10 litres (17.6 pints)

5 litres (8.8 pints)

0

Nineteen tennis courts cover an area of 4,959 sq m (53,380 sq ft).

Adult drawn to scale of tennis courts

Curled up in the womb, a 40-week-old foetus is about as big as a rugby ball.

Size for size, a baby's head is twice as big as an adult's. A baby's head is about a quarter of the length of its body, an adult's about an eighth.

From fertilized egg to full-size foetus

Before you are even born, your body undergoes a phenomenal increase in size. You begin life as a fertilized egg no bigger than the full stop that ends this sentence. After four weeks of rapid growth you are about as big as a pea – at this stage you are called an embryo. After eight weeks you are about the size of a brazil nut – from then on you are called a foetus. Finally, after 40 weeks you are fully developed and, curled up inside your mother's womb, are about the size of a rugby ball.

Newly fertilized human egg (actual size): about 0.14 mm (0.006 in) long

Four-week-old embryo (actual size): about 7 mm (0.3 in) long

Eight-week-old foetus (actual size): about 3 cm (1.2 in) long

Forty-week-old foetus (actual size): about 50 cm (20 in) long

Bone-size baby

The average newborn baby measures about 50 cm (20 in) from head to toe, which is about the same size as the average adult's thighbone. After growing so rapidly inside your mother's body, it takes you about 18 years to grow from a newborn baby into a full-size adult (see page 53).

Newborn baby: 50 cm (20 in)

Adult's thighbone: 50 cm (20 in)

Straight from the horse's mouth?

Stretched out, an adult's intestines are about 7.5 m (25 ft) long in total, while those of a fully grown horse add up to an amazing 27 m (89 ft) – almost four times as long. Luckily, the intestines are curled up inside the body, otherwise there would be some very odd-looking people and horses around, as shown below.

The large intestine of a fully grown horse is about 6 m (20 ft) long.

Normal horse

The small intestine of a fully grown horse is about 21 m (69 ft) long.

The small intestine of an adult human is about 6 m (20 ft) long.

The large intestine of an adult human is about 1.5 m (5 ft) long.

Normal human

57

The 1.5-mm (0.06-in) common flea can jump almost 20 cm (8 in) high – equivalent to a 1.75-m (5-ft 9-in) man jumping 227.5 m (746 ft).

HUMANS AND ANIMALS

ARE HUMANS SUPERIOR to animals? When it comes to brain power, we like to think that we are well ahead of even the most intelligent animals, such as dolphins. Two ways in which we are clearly superior are our use of tools, and our ability to talk. Plainly, however, plenty of creatures are much stronger than we are – no human could ever beat a gorilla in a wrestling match. Nor are we necessarily physically superior to creatures that are much smaller than we are. Size for size, ants are even stronger than gorillas. Nor can we survive in such extreme environments as many animals can. Birds fly at altitudes where we would be unable to breathe, while sperm whales can swim at depths where the water pressure would quickly kill us. Only with the aid of machines can we safely venture into the worlds of these animals.

Enjoying the high life

Although many mountaineers have climbed the highest mountain in the world, Mt Everest, without special breathing equipment, humans are only able to ascend to greater heights in aircraft and balloons with the aid of oxygen. Some birds, however, appear to be able to fly at almost one-and-a-half times the height of Everest without difficulty. But the really high fliers are airborne bacteria, which have been found at almost five times the height of Everest.

Deep beneath the waves

Most humans cannot hold their breath underwater for more than a few seconds. Scuba divers cannot safely dive much below about 50 m (164 ft), because of the dangerous effects on the body of high water pressure. But some sea animals have no such problems. Sperm whales hunting giant squid might dive six times as deep as the Empire State Building is tall – holding their breath underwater for hours at a time.

Tail feathers top hair

There are several recorded examples of women who have been able to grow their hair to more than twice their height. This achievement falls well short of the remarkable Japanese Phoenix fowl, however, which has been selectively bred over the years to grow longer and longer tail feathers – up to almost twice as long as a giraffe is tall.

Human hair grows about 1.2 cm (0.5 in) a month. Uncut, it usually stops growing when it is 60-90 cm (2-3 ft) long. But some women are able to grow their hair to nearly 4 m (13 ft).

The mighty ant

A human can squash an ant under a fingertip but, size for size, ants are much stronger than we are. An ant can lift and carry about 50 times its own body weight. This is equivalent to a 64-kg (141-lb) man lifting 3,200 kg (7,055 lb) – about the weight of three family cars.

If humans were as strong as ants, a 64-kg (141-lb) man would be able to lift three family cars above his head.

Musclebound gorillas

Gorillas are up to eight times stronger than humans. If gorillas lifted weights, the world weightlifting record might be increased from 266 kg (586 lb) to 2,128 kg (4,691 lb).

In 1988, Leonid Taranenko, of the then Soviet Union, set a new world weightlifting record for men of 266 kg (586 lb) – equivalent to lifting four 64-kg (141-lb) men above his head.

If gorillas lifted weights, they might be able to lift more than 2 tonnes (2 tons) – about the weight of two family cars.

In 1992, Li Yajuan, of China, set a new world weightlifting record for women of 150 kg (331 lb).

The longest recorded tail feathers on a Japanese Phoenix fowl were an amazing 10.6 m (34 ft 9 in).

The giraffe is the tallest animal in the world, growing up to 5.8 m (19 ft) in height.

Migrating whooper swans sometimes fly at more than 8,230 m (27,000 ft). But the record for high flying goes to the Rüppell's griffon, a kind of vulture. In 1973, above the Ivory Coast, a Rüppell's griffon collided with an aircraft at 11.278 m (37,000 ft).

Mt Everest, in the Himalayas, is 8,848 m (29,028 ft) high. It was first climbed in 1953, by Edmund Hillary and Sherpa Tenzing.

Toads live at up to 8,000 m (26,247 ft) in the Himalayas.

Jumping spiders have been found living at 6,706 m (22,000 ft) on Mt Everest.

Yaks are frequently seen at 6,000 m (19,685 ft) or more in the Himalayas.

Airborne bacteria have been found alive and well at a height of 41,000 m (134,514 ft).

12,000 m (39,370 ft)	
11,000 m (36,089 ft)	
10,000 m (32,808 ft)	
9,000 m (29,528 ft)	
8,000 m (26,247 ft)	
7,000 m (22,966 ft)	
6,000 m (19,685 ft)	
5,000 m (16,404 ft)	

Depth scale (left)

3,000 m (9,843 ft)
2,000 m (6,562 ft)
1,000 m (3,281 ft)
0

1,000 m (3,281 ft)
2,000 m (6,562 ft)
3,000 m (9,843 ft)
4,000 m (13,123 ft)
5,000 m (16,404 ft)
6,000 m (19,685 ft)
7,000 m (22,966 ft)
8,000 m (26,247 ft)
9,000 m (29,528 ft)
10,000 m (32,808 ft)

Hi there, landlubbers! I can hold my breath for two minutes or more, but only because I have had years of training, so don't try this at home!

Holding their breath, pearl divers can descend 15 m (49 ft), and sponge divers twice this depth.

Antarctic Emperor penguins can dive to 265 m (869 ft).

Sperm whales regularly dive to 1,200 m (3,937 ft), and possibly to 2,400 m (7,874 ft) or more at times – a depth more than six times the height of New York's Empire State Building.

Some brotulid fish live 8,300 m (27,231 ft) deep in the sea.

Shrimp-like amphipods live at 10,500 m (34,449 ft) in the depths of the Pacific Ocean.

Sea urchins live near the bottom of the Marianas Trench, in the Pacific Ocean, at 10,710 m (35,138 ft).

Koala likes its kip

On average, humans need eight hours of sleep a day. The amount of sleep that animals need varies enormously. Shrews never sleep, except when hibernating, while koala bears are seldom awake. Between these extremes, cats like nothing better than to curl up in front of a warm fire. The clocks show the average length of time each animal sleeps in a day.

Koala bear — 22:00
Gorilla — 12:00
Sloth — 20:00
Human — 08:00
Giant armadillo — 18:05
Asian elephant — 03:54
Cat — 14:30
Sheep — 03:48
Pig — 13:00
Shrew — 00:00

High achievers

Top high jumpers can leap almost as high as the Australian red kangaroo – yet are leaden-footed compared with some animals. While we struggle to jump above head-high – even with a run-up – the klipspringer antelope of southern Africa can jump 15 times its height. But fleas are the stars – from rest, a common flea can hop as high as 130 times its body size.

The 50-cm (20-in) tall klipspringer can jump 7.5 m (25 ft) high – equivalent to a 1.75-m (5-ft 9-in) man jumping 26.25 m (86 ft).

The 2-m (6.5-ft) tall red kangaroo can spring 3 m (10 ft) into the air.

In 1989, Javier Sotomayor, of Cuba, set a new world high jump record for men by clearing 2.44 m (8 ft 0.5 in).

Bulgarian Stefka Kostadinova set a new women's world high jump record of 2.09 m (6 ft 10.25 in) in 1987.

A 10-cm (4-in) long jerboa, or desert rat, can jump 4.5 m (15 ft) – 45 times its body length.

Leaps and bounds

Like top high jumpers, top long jumpers can almost match the red kangaroo – with a fast run-up. But several much smaller animals can jump much further in relation to their size – and from a standing start. As in the high jump, fleas are the champions.

In 1991, Mike Powell, of the USA, set a new world long jump record for men with a leap of 8.95 m (29 ft 4.5 in).

Red kangaroos can cover 9 m (30 ft) or more in one bound.

A 30-cm (12-in) long goliath frog can jump 3 m (10 ft) – 10 times its body length.

A 1.75-m (5-ft 9-in) man jumping 10 times his body length would cover 17.5 m (57 ft).

A 25-cm (10-in) long Asian grasshopper can jump 4.5 m (15 ft) – 18 body lengths.

A 1.75-m (5-ft 9-in) man jumping 18 times his body length would cover 31.5 m (103 ft).

A 1.75-m (5-ft 9-in) man jumping 45 times his body length would cover 78.75 m (258 ft).

A 1.75-m (5-ft 9-in) man jumping 220 times his body length would cover 385 m (1,263 ft).

Fleas jump the furthest

The amazing jumping abilities of *Pulex irritans*, the common flea, were measured in a series of experiments conducted by M. B. Mitzmain, a US scientist, in 1910.

A 1.5-mm (0.06-in) common flea can jump up to 33 cm (13 in) lengthways – 220 times its body size.

Scale markers (leaps section)
10 m (33 ft)
20 m (66 ft)
30 m (98 ft)
40 m (131 ft)
80 m (262 ft)
400 m (1,312 ft)

10 m (33 ft)
20 m (66 ft)
60 m (197 ft)
300 m (984 ft)

10 m (33 ft)
40 m (131 ft)
200 m (656 ft)

20 m (66 ft)
100 m (328 ft)

33 cm (13 in)

0

INDEX

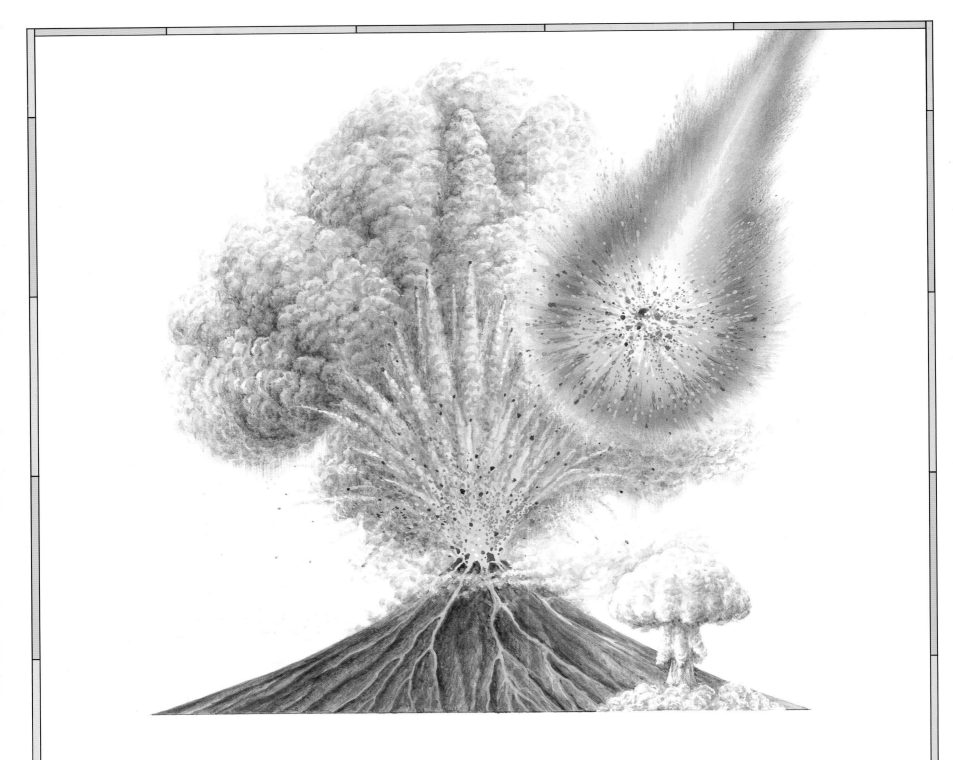

ACKNOWLEDGMENTS

Dorling Kindersley would like to thank
the following for helping with this book –

Design: Jo Earl; Jim Miles; Sheilagh Noble

Editorial: Terry Martin; Richard Platt; Phil Wilkinson

Research: Professor John Allen; Amateur Yacht Research Society;
Cameron Balloons; Carluccio's; Chicago Bridge & Iron Company;
Dr Peter Cotgreave, London Zoo; Edificio Petróleos de Venezuela;
Robert Graham; Hapag Lloyd; Kitty Hauser; Esther Labi;
Lindstrand Balloons; Lloyd's List; Keith Lye;
Natural History Museum; P & O; Steve Parker;
Royal Botanic Gardens, Kew;
Silja Shipping; World Sailing Records